PREYING MANTIS

POLITICAL COMMENTARY

VOLUME II

Francis Oisaghaede Egbokhare

Francis Egbokhare

Preying Mantis (Volume II)

A NOTE FROM THE AUTHOR

The Praying Mantis is an insect. In traditional mythology, there are many superstitious beliefs about it. It is a mysterious and fear inspiring insect. Children are afraid to kill it to avoid unpleasant circumstances. The slow movement is its mystery. Growing up in the village, I reverenced the praying mantis. What many adults do not know is even then, a number of children would secretly kill the praying mantis and watch it discharge its larvae. Children broke many taboos in the village setting. Nevertheless, when adults witness or hear about any taboo being broken they take children through some form of cleansing. The praying mantis became for me a symbol of control, rigidity of traditions, unquestioning loyalty and blind faith. In 2004, when the Nigerian Tribune asked me to write a column for their Sunday edition, I thought of a way to be obvious while being obscure. I also wanted to be critical in a humorous and respectful way because the Nigerian media in my opinion was full of aggressive and abusive writers at the time. I thought I should prey on the prevailing mindset without denigrating the belief system. Preying Mantis stood for two values: change and reflection. The title is a pun on the insect Praying Mantis, except that I chose to prey on old, worn out and beaten paths.

The insect in my culture is a symbol of meditation and sobriety. As I expected, many people never noticed the difference in spelling or concept. In the four years that I wrote the column, I wrote on politics, politically exposed persons, culture, society and any topic that was trending. The materials are organised in two volumes, Socio-cultural Commentary and

Political Commentary. The first volume has ninety-nine chapters while the second one has sixty-one chapters. The chapters are short and readable, as one would expect from a column that restricted one to less than half a page. We have chosen to organise the materials thematically instead of chronologically in order to give it the feel of a book and distil out the thought pattern or message of the writer. Nevertheless, we dated the articles in many cases. Dating will help the political articles read better because it will facilitate the reconstruction of the context of the essay. There is a glossary of names and terms that would be unfamiliar to the international readers and many young Nigerians. These terms are italicised and presented in alphabetical order in the glossary.

As one would expect, a lot has happened since 2009 when the last piece was written. The major actors are all gone and technology has transformed the world beyond recognition. You would agree that the average human has changed little fundamentally in the most important areas of life. Prejudices are widening, wars persist and are expanding, bigotry is finding new expressions and man is still a merchant of error and injustice. Let me conclude with some extracts from chapter ninety-nine of volume one entitled, Signing Off.

…What has length of time to do with life if there is no impact? Every position is for an appointed time. The fact that we are applauded is not enough reason why we must begin to think of ourselves more highly than we ought to. Better people are yet to be born and more glorious things will be done after we are gone. I know of a man who was snatched from the jaws of death and made the ruler of a country to try him out if his conversion was real. For a while, he remembered his God and for a while longer he remembered his women. Then a little while longer after his memory recessed, he sought the glories of men and enjoyed the adulation of Hippocrates. He thought in his heart to build a castle to heaven and would have climbed up high but that God in his mercy caused him to fall while he could still be saved. We must be humble enough to recognize that we are a piece in the puzzle of life.

I take responsibility for all the opinions expressed in these volumes. I am grateful to the Nigerian Tribune for giving me space to express my thoughts freely. I dedicate the volumes to it.

Francis Oisaghaede Egbokhare

Ibadan

16 December, 2015

Table of Contents

CHAPTER ONE

THE DEVIL'S ALTERNATIVE

These times remind me of the puzzle which people often throw up as a way of resolving the dilemma of love. It goes like this; if your mother and your wife are drowning, who of the two would you save. I am always amused at the answers that people give because they assume that such actions are driven by rational behaviour. What I will do may depend on a number of variables none of which may remotely have anything to do with love for one or the other. I think I will not save any of them. I pause a while to allow your imagination some excursion into condemnation. Actually, I will not because I cannot swim. So, it will be most irrational of me to compound the tragedy by committing suicide. Sometimes, in order to express a dilemma, one may say that he is between the devil and the deep blue sea. For me there ought to be no dilemma in that except for the sentiments which our religious persuasion may foist on us. Non-religious people will not have this dilemma at all, because the practical needs of survival will make the Devil's option the most realistic. We sometimes hear that the devil you know is better than the saint you do not know. I don't think that there is a greater fallacy than this. A saint is a saint and a devil is a devil. Someone has described the political situation in Oyo state as a case of two Governors and one referee. I don't think so. It reminds me of the lunatic who set fire to the village and when he was confronted, he said he only set fire to a spot. He refused to accept responsibility for the rest of the village. Obasanjo and Adedibu remind me of the Hausa entertainers who go about with Hyenas and baboons on a leash.

Work it out for yourself. Can you believe that Obasanjo is actually playing tricks on Nigerians? He actually wants Atiku to be elected. Just a couple of weeks ago he became the director of Atiku

Campaign Organisation. Six months ago, Atiku was dead politically until Obasanjo revived his political ambition through uncontrolled assault and indiscretions of un-presidential proportions. Many Nigerians now believe in an Atiku presidency. Some who do not care about the man have found in him an opportunity to get rid of whatever Obasanjo stands for. Many now describe him as courageous. Quite a number will cast sympathy votes for him. Every time Atiku is attacked he gains new advantage. He has used the courts effectively to create the impression that he is being unjustly treated. Is Atiku corrupt? I think Nigerians believe that most politicians are thieves. They have every reason to believe so. I f the reason for condemning him is that he stole some money, Many Nigerians are also pointing to signs of affluence in Mr President. In spite of Ribadu's claim to the contrary, the sudden change in fortune of Obasanjo farms, his acquisition of new farms while still serving and the Transcorp issue have lead Nigerians to believe that Mr President and his Vice are actually brothers running the same business. Apart from that, there are a few people in the presidency who Nigerians believe greased their palms with public funds, yet no one is bothering them at all. So if Oga hates thieves, why are some thieves being protected? I understand that the dichotomy between white witches and black witches has now found relevance in the presidency. If you are a white or good thief, you are not troubled. But all black thieves are hunted down by EFCC. I feel sorry for Ribadu, because he is working in a difficult political terrain. He has to suffer some indignities and pretend a little bit until an opportune time. Moreover, except he gets a petition, he is not likely going to be able to do anything on mere suspicion.

Even where there is a petition, if the right documents are not available, what can he do? It is easy to manipulate him by using other security agencies to generate the petitions against enemies of government. Is it really true that Mr Yar Adua wears a diaper? All kinds of things are flying around about him. Already he has been labelled as OBj's dog. He apparently does not try to shake this off. I guess he believes that campaigning is a mere formality. He is a president in waiting. After hearing Obj lie that 2003 elections were not rigged, I made up my mind that 2007 will be free but not fair. What kind of president is Yar Adua going to be? His only qualification to date appears to be that he saved 6 billion naira in Katsina. He appears to be clean. But I think his greatest asset is that he is a civilian and a graduate. The PDP doesn't seem to recognize that Nigerians are tired of the military. Buhari's past will surely hunt him in the elections. There are many people who will not easily forget his draconian rule. The failure of character in Obj appears to be making a hero of all comers. If Buhari is considered a religious fanatic, he will have a partner in Yar Adua. If Yar Adua is clean as regards corruption, perhaps, Buhari is considered to be squeaky clean. He, more than any of the other candidates has what it takes to fight corruption. Neither Atiku nor Yar Aua will do better than Obj in this respect. An Atiku victory will see Obj back to his address in jail, but what will happen to the thieving Governors and politicians around him? What will happen to EFCC? Will Yar Adua be able to extricate himself from the PDP mafia? Not likely. If they continue in the current overdrive, in two years they will all be spent and used up. Can he probe Obj's administration? Not likely. We are going to have more of the same thing and less of governance. One thing I will like to see after the elections is a virile opposition. This will happen only if the PDP loses. If it wins again we will see a lot of carpet crossing and begging for forgiveness. If either AC or ANPP wins we should expect also intra party squabbles for the next four years at least. There is always a problem when thieves try to share loot. Let no Nigerian be deceived, no fundamental restructuring of the polity will take place unless there is a catharsis. From the conduct of the opposition so far, it is clear that the difference between the parties may be likened to the difference between guguru and popcorn. I will leave you with a joke. A man was caught impersonating Nuhu Ribadu. He was arraigned in court. His charges were read and he pled not guilty. He claimed that the police did not pay enough attention to the spelling of his name which according to him ends with an "n". His name is Ribadun, meaning Riba is sweet.

18 February, 2007

CHAPTER TWO

POSTURING FOR 2007

Politics is everything in Nigeria. There's no business as profitable. In fact, it is doubtful if any other business goes on. The Senate President alluded to this when he referred to our distinguished senators as investors. What we call politics actually is a struggle for control and advantage. It applies at the micro, class and the ethnic levels. The only real or meaningful business run by government is the sale of crude oil. As it was in those days with the sale of slaves and later produce, the person who controls power controls the commodity. Everyone is forced to make friends with him. The Nigerian business environments sounds like the apocalyptic beast. Anyone who wishes to survive must carry the mark of the beast. Today, PDP is Nigeria's beast and it controls the oil revenue. You either join PDP or face the consequence. Nigeria's politics is not likely going to change significantly until the private sector is grown significantly. Until such a time when politics is not the main business of Nigerians, we are in trouble. To date, the Nigerian economy is like an orange. There is no logical point to divide the private sector from the pubic sector.

One must understand the agitations for power shift in this light. What Nigerians are asking for is that each ethnic group should be given an opportunity to control oil and power. Then, whoever is in charge can invite his kinsmen and friends to *come and chop*. Don't mind the whole cry of marginalization and cry for justice. Truth is, people are simply crying for advantage. Once they get the upper hand they begin to sound a different tune. What has become of the cry for a national conference; sovereign, or suffering. Those who shouted the loudest and cried themselves hoarse now only manage to whimper it because they are in a position to *chop.*

Nigeria is really not a country serious about change, the educated elite is irresponsible. The race to 2007 has started indeed and the Yoruba appear to have accepted the principle of rotation. But they are not saying whether Ndigbo deserves to have a shot at the presidency or not. Obviously, the Yoruba have benefited from power shift. They have also lost the moral edge and argument over the rest of Nigeria. After Obasanjo, no one again may blame the Hausa-Fulani for the woes of Nigeria. It is clear now that the Yoruba can also produce after our kind. We have always had rulers but never a leader. I know as the argument goes, Obasanjo means well. Who cares, what we want is results. The argument in the past was that northern rulers failed because of their lack of solid education. Now we have a leader from elsewhere who we hope will not end with a negative evaluation. There is still time. If the regional factor is not bandied, it is the poor education of successive leaders that is now emphasized. I hope our next leader is a professor of politics and philosophy with minor in religion and sociology. Of course he or she will also fail. Perhaps Nigerians will begin to ask the real questions thereafter. There is no way any person or group will succeed under the present structure. I think we now need to demystify the Igbo. We need to do this quickly to stop this name-calling and stone throwing at innocent ethnic groups. We need an Igbo president in 2007.

The Igbo appear really serious about 2007. With Rochas Okorocha building bridges across the Niger and shaking hands with the sword, one can almost say *no shaking* in 2007. If we were to go by number of cars, I think he has made it already. The Igbo for 2007 campaign has gathered momentum. One is however surprised that Ndigbo are boiling mainly on television and on the pages of newspapers. Unfortunately, the voters are not on TV and do not read newspapers. Besides, those who fix elections don't care about such things. *Rochas* and *Ebeano* are quite a spectacle. These two have set up homes in NTA. They are spending so much that one is afraid that by the time politicians are ready to sell, they won't have enough money to buy. If *Chimaroke* has done so well in *Enugu* as he claims, he doesn't need to beam those programmes to people who do not care about what on earth goes on in Enugu. From what one hears, the state has changed a lot on TV. One is inclined to believe that all the shenanigans is for the vice presidency. If this is true, then it is a pity.

The South-South clowns are really quiet these days. I think the fact that the end of the road is in sight. The Edo man has played his last card. That's how far he will go farther or no farther. With the Fixer seeking the position for his ward, he may not even have a say. The Delta man has grown up. Politics is not about big mouth or big money only. After 2007 if he survives the courts, he will have to face his business. He is set for a less powerful role. As he will soon learn, even if you put someone there, he will show youthat he has the key. The Bayelsa man should take enough pictures so as to remember that he once played politics.

The Rivers man has been a very good boy to OBJ. If the latter still calls the shot, then he may get a chance to remain in the limelight. I think he is angling for the number two job as are his other colleagues. One thing one will not miss if they drop out of the scene is their clown costumes.

Arewa and Ndigbo and their retinue of agents are rowdy with claims of the right to power. The groups have nothing to offer Nigeria, no matter how one views it. They are simply groups formed by individuals to position themselves and posture for power. Apart from criticizing leadership from other ethnic groups, it is unheard of for them to criticize their own people let alone governments in their ethnic area for obvious corruption, injustices and maladministration.

Nigeria is a country of contradictions. After annulling June 12, Babangida appears to be set for a second coming. Atiku on his part in recent times has been abroad on pilgrimage to Uncle Sam and

Uncle Blair. Of course some evidences of this are new rhetoric of mainstream political and economic paradigms. One is not quite sure which of the 2007 gladiators is going to happen on Nigeria. It was rather curious to hear OBJ say that he knows who will not succeed him. I hope politicians are listening. How could he possibly know, a mortal man? Does he have Herod Syndrome or does the cap fit him? Even if one were to dismiss this as a typical Baba-ism, one cannot ignore the suggestion that 2007 has been fixed.

I had a hard time believing that Babangida was really interested in a second coming until I noticed that he has taken up the pastime of attending children's birthday parties and funerals. He's been also to weddings and naming ceremonies. Uncharacteristically, he has become loquacious. We are waiting for that great story of how the devil got him to annul June 12. There will be surely positive development from his second coming. One thing is sure that our corruption lexicon will expand and we may witness innovations in the art of fixing. I think that we will be saved the spectacle of bleached first and second ladies. A Babangida presidency will leave us in no doubt who is first lady. Can we say that about an Atiku presidency? We may introduce the concept of the office of the second and third ladies.

22 August, 2004

CHAPTER THREE

THE FALL OF EL RUFAI

Senate has had a sweet revenge on one of its most ardent critics. Until recently, I had thought of El Rufai as someone who is rigidly principled and supremely transparent. When he called senators fools, I was shocked; but I was heart-broken at the cheap way he was demystified. I couldn't believe that like a tame dog, he could so easily tuck his tail between his legs. Yes, it is a sign of strength to be wrong and so admit. It is perhaps greater virtue to bow out in the place of dishonour. Frankly, I expected El Rufai to apologize, because he was disrespectful. I also expected him to resign because his conduct fell far beneath the expectation of his office. If he truly hold senators to such scorn, then he ought to have defied them by resigning. But whoever resigns in Nigeria?

Mallam Nasir El Rufai is one of those people in the present Government that many Nigerians have come to love. From his days in the Bureau for Public Enterprise to his present appointment as the Minister of the FCT, he has cut an image of a fearless and honest Nigerian. I actually like the man. I think that he became too secure in the corridors of power. He may have learnt one or two lessons from the current "sack and begging shame". What was going on in his mind when he called Senators fools? This Senate as a matter of fact is roundly believed by Nigerians to be puppets in the hands of the executive. Most of them were appointed to Senate by Election. Many would not have been nowhere near they are but for OBJ. This notwithstanding, it is unpardonable for a Minister to so deride this very important institution of governance. Well, nothing is impossible in Nigeria. If you know how to beg in Nigeria, there is no problem you cannot solve. When a governor and a certain party big wig had a serious problem, the Governor went to the palace of a traditional ruler to beg. Political parties and

Traditional Rulers provide the best begging platforms in Nigeria. I think the floor of Senate has now joined the platforms.

I honestly expected El Rufai to resign his appointment instead of crawling back to Senators and blaming the devil. If he resigned, he may have had to answer for the charges of corruption against him. It is difficult now to determine if his grovelling is as a result of penitence or an attempt to cover up allegations against him. I honestly hope he comes clean.

My worry now is that Abuja master plan has been compromised finally. Hasn't Rufai been neutralized? Hasn't the wind been taken out his sail? He may now have to settle down to normal Government – A la Abuja since his fangs has been plucked out. He is now a tamed bull.

If it turns out that he was actually guilty of corruption – which I hope not because Nigeria is in desperate need of true heroes – we will then need to look more carefully at the activities of our popular leaders. A very popular leader may in fact be dangerous because in his/her peak period, he/she can get away with illegalities because of the sheer force of positive public opinions. Hitherto, who dared to criticize El Rufai in the papers? A country ought to be run by structures, processes and laws not the charm of personalities.

19 September, 2004

CHAPTER FOUR

ZEAL WITHOUT WISDOM

Tribune of Saturday 6, November 2004 has a photograph of Mr. Mainstream Politics with mouth open as usual. I don't remember seeing a picture of him with his mouth closed. The headline reads, "We'll get rid of Tinubu". There was also another headline, this time it was Fani Kayode's picture but he had his mouth shut, quite unexpectedly. Mr Mainstream is a zealous and committed politician who is sometimes given to exaggeration and blind support. He once stated that the 2003 elections were free and fair when even blind people noticed the massive rigging. He has done it again trying to justify the rise in the cost of fuel.

On page 34 of Saturday Tribune, of November, he stated that "in America a litre of fuel is sold for over two dollars and in England, it is about two something. Democracy is about 200 years old, we are just about five years old and we are just coming to terms with realities of our situation because these are things that should have been put in place".

First, it is necessary to point out that in America, a litre or fuel does not sell for $2. A gallon of fuel sells for about $2 depending on which part of the U.S. you are. A gallon has about 4 litres. Second, he needs to know that Europe and America subsidize agriculture heavily and they have all kinds of unfair trade practices which prevent developing nations from competing.

Finally, democracy is not a religion; Mr Mainstream should stop behaving like a **Babalawo** or priest of democracy. He is a privileged Nigerian who does not know what goes on in the markets. People are complaining because they are suffering not because they love being unruly.

I don't know why PDP cannot leave Tinubu alone in Lagos and face their business in several other states where they have crises such as Plateau, Delta, Anambra, Rivers, etc. How can they get rid of Tinubu since he is running his last term? The irony of Nigeria is that those who fail an exam get rewarded with leadership positions. If people lose elections and are appointed ministers to compensate them it is bad enough. For them now to seek to dominate elected officials is embarrassing, to say the least. If Ibori can be, why can't Tinubu? If Fayose is allowed to thrive, why not Tinubu? Equal measures, that is democracy.

28 November 2004

CHAPTER FIVE

DANCING WITH WOLVES

In contemporary Nigeria, Leadership is a misnomer, what we have is *Leaderhood.* Everything is person centred not issues driven. If issues are mentioned, the issue is money. Politics is unfortunately equated with intrigues; it is a matter of struggle for position as a means to material fulfilment. Under this condition, there is absolutely no room for dissent. To disagree is to be disloyal; to express it is equal to treason. The Leader is the state and the state is an expression of the leader. The only kind of governance that can work in this condition is not democracy but sycophancy – a government by praise singers, for praise singers and of praise singing.

The newspapers are filled with reports and comments of those who are gloating over *Ogbeh*'s resignation. Some would want us to believe that the man is corrupt. I agree that he is. It would be a misnomer to have a PDP big wig who is not a corruption kingpin. Pardon my cynicism. But it can't be that he resigned to prove a point or pave the way for a probe. After all, he shared pounded yam with OBJ and both of them hugged and forgave each other in the typical triviality that defines our home video tragedy called Nigeria.

I think the issue is 2007. We must remember that fools die and the wise live to tell their story. Only the stupid did not foresee that PDP had to go through this. First, from the last convention, Mr. V.P. miscalculated. If he is as astute as some claim he is, he should have known the implications of cutting a deal with a man after rubbing his nose in shit. You don't go that far in war, as a soldier, close to victory and sign a peace deal. Atiku is not a soldier, but there are lessons to learn from the convention. OBJ is a soldier; he has forgiven but not forgotten. You do not leave an adversary strong, you eliminate him. The odds are now stacked in his favour. He has nothing to lose; but his ego is huge and he needs the last laugh and the last say. There are many rabble-rousers in Nigerian political scene. They know nothing about politics save that they paid too much money for bribes. Politics is not about ideas in this country, it is a function of how much you control in capital. There are things money cannot do and we are beginning to get there. OBJ needs desperately to call the shots. He needs the shot if he has to have a life after 2007 – third term or not.

The mistake is that many people are deceived by OBJs religious image. I don't think he remembers God when he plays his politics. Not many people do, not even Prof. Jerry Gana. There is another mistake being made, and that is that PDP will die or weaken with the formation of another party by so called progressives. This is poor reasoning. PDP is not strong or weak by its membership. It is strong or weak by the degree to which it controls the nation's power and resources. That is in the hands of OBJ and his friends. Second issue is that parties do not win or lose elections because they have smatter politicians. They win or lose because they control INEC and the police. The Presidency controls both. So OBJ does not need these so-called progressives who are not better than him anyway. They need him. If it is true that Atiku has a problem with OBJ; he has a problem indeed. Just wait for appointments to Boards to be made and you will feel sorry for him. There will be a lot of carpets to cross. If OBJ is smart, he will not fill all the slots at one go. He should use the remaining slots as bait. If he is the good soldier I think he is after getting them to do what he wants, he will disappoint them. Lesson – never honour a deal with your adversary. Nigerian politics is running on the principles of war not of peace. Soldiers win war not civilians. I have an advice for *Atiku*. He should play the loyal wife who insists that she will keep her home in spite of being maltreated by her husband. Since men are always prone to the ways of the flesh, the woman could still have her laugh. Things happen to a lot of men by the hands of their wives and people never know about it. If he remains in PDP, there is no way he can be totally ignored. At least he can play the spoiler if he can't be president. If he leaves PDP, he will not be president and he will not be relevant.

I think Nigerians should be happy at what is happening in PDP. Their attitude should not be to take sides – in fact, we should pray for more crises. PDP is like the biblical Babylon the great. Except it falls, the salvation of the people will not come. *PDP* represents a thinking and a class. Significant things are happening and we are not taking note. The sentencing of the Navy Admirals is an indication indeed that we have changed from one class of oppressors to the other. We have shifted power from military oppression to civilian oppression but we are not yet in a democracy. Democracy will come when power shifts to the people. The power shift that we all are unfortunately clamouring for is the one that will perpetuate oppression. The real shift will transfer power to the people and thereby solve the problem of dominance. The common Nigerian has shown that he is not a slave to religion or ethnicity. Our political elites use these as negotiating instruments for their own gains. In 1993, Nigerians voted en masse for Abiola. What we need to ensure power shift is to put down structures and programme that will lead to credible elections. Once the people can exercise their rights to hire and fire the politicians, sanity will prevail and parties like PDP will give way. The other point is that we must negotiate our relationship as a people otherwise some people will bear unfair burdens.

30 January, 2005

CHAPTER SIX

PLAYING GOD

I am just put off when I see some men playing God. First, there are those who feel that Nigerians should be grateful to them for all the good wisdom that they are applying to our economy. There, are others who are so worried about their legacies and those who will succeed them, that they wish to toy with the political process. They have started to think that they alone are good enough to succeed themselves. We hear statements like, "we know those who will succeed us".

How can a man be so sure! We need to begin to understand that in a system where the right structures and systems are not in place, anything can happen. It is so much easier to allow processes take care of things than for men to try manipulate things. For those who feel so sure of their successors. I will remind you that Shakespeare says "there is no art to find the minds construction in the face". But there are means of ensuring that some kinds of mindless constructions are never realized. Instead of Mr President worrying so much about who succeeds him, he should worry about conducting a credible election. This is his final chance. One is particularly disturbed that he has hijacked the national conference and pooh poohed it.

Why will one man nominate more than 10% of the participants? Why are they so scared of the truth? To determine abinitio that some areas are no go areas is to sabotage the conference from the beginning. As I sat looking at a governor so zealously stating why some areas are no go, I asked myself who appointed them to decide for us what we should talk about. We know many of these people. They are part of the problem. If we cannot talk about religion and decide if we should remain as one people, I wonder what else there is to discuss. This morbid fear that Nigeria will disintegrate at a conference because people want to argue if it is worth it being a people beats me hollow. What would one rather have a war? I hear all these talk by bloated politicians about how they will defend the unity of Nigeria with their blood and I ask myself which blood and which unity! There is no unity! We are not a nation much less a people. The issue is how we emerge as a nation. Moreover, it is pure lip service and in fact it is, dishonest of these thieves to make these claims. We are here bearing the consequence of their misrule, bearing the burden of their fraud, we die daily in the name of unity and they are waiting for that future when their infected blood will become useful. People do not believe that Nigeria can fight another war. It is exactly when people think that war is remote that there is the greatest threat of war. "When you hear peace, suddenly the end will come." I don't pray for war, but those who will refuse dialogue should make arrangement for violence.

6 February, 2005

CHAPTER SEVEN

EDO: TRULY THE HEARTBEAT

Edo State is a peculiar place in many respects. All over the world, the name Edo is reminiscent of the ancient Benin Kingdom known for its Bronze Works. The state is rich in culture and history. The better known history is that of ancient Benin. Yet Benin is just a section of a much more diverse and interesting place. The term Edo has its origin from the term "do", a popular greeting form for "hello" found in Urhobo, Isoko, Pidgin and among the Owan people. Edo literally means people who greet "do". Benin historians will disagree with this. They prefer to trace the origin of the name, curiously to a loyal slave of one of the kings. No matter the source of the name, the Benins have appropriated the name to themselves.

The Benin in Edo State neither distinguish between other Edo people and foreigners, except that politically, they are compelled to accommodate them within the geographical expression. Most groups trace their origins to the kingdom days; but in actual fact, from other evidence, this refers to a period of migration. The Edo area is peopled by aboriginals whose closest relatives are in the Northern hills. There are migrant elements from Nupe, Igala, Igbira and other groups.

In fact, the kingdom area is much more recently settled than the areas around the Northern hills. It is the Benins who are to be derived from the Northern people. But as we all know, history and its interpretation favours the larger and more influential group. That is the sad story.

The contemporary history of Edo is a sad story. We can begin the fall of Edo from the creation of Delta State and the rise of the Benins to pre-eminence. In the old Bendel, the equally popular and assertive Urhobo, the Isoko, etc. created necessary balance which made it necessary for the Edo-Benin to accommodate smaller more related groups in its calculation.

The politics today favour the more numerically strong Benin group. And among them, the moneybags have taken over leadership from such fearless people as *AIR-Iyare* and dynamic leaders like *Ogbemudia*. The fall of the intellectual class, coincides with the commanding political influence of this group and the *exemption factor*. The growing political stature of Chief Gabriel Igbinedion started during the time of Jerry Useni. Since then, he has become the single most important factor in Edo State politics and his family is trying to be what Bush's family has been in American politics. There is no doubt about the fact that they rule and reign in Edo but it is clear that in the larger Nigeria, they do not have the means or clout or wherewithal to overcome the formidable obstacles. Has the exemption factor led to positive developments in Edo State politics? I don't believe so.

Within the Benin setting, it is doubtful that they command a majority. This is the tragedy in fact. Equating the inequalities in Edo State politics with the insatiable appetite of the Benin for dominance is an unfortunate perception deriving only from the fact that those who reign are Benin. They do not in fact, reign by popular mandate of the Benin themselves. Chief Lucky Igbinedion may not have the native wisdom of his father; but he certainly has mastered his elementary politics of Edo.

Two factors are important in Edo politics. One, you need the *Agbero* to control the ground troops, especially in Benin City. Second, you need *Chief Tony Anenih* to control PDP politics, and maintain strong presence at the National from where elections are rigged.

The latter factor was particularly important in Igbinedion's second term bid. Once he secured it, as one expected, it was no longer necessary for him to bow to Chief Anenih, especially as it is now clear that Anenih wants his son to be the next Governor.

The process of demystifying Anenih is a project in a calculation inspired by the tussle for succession towards 2007. Will Anenih Junior or Bright Igbinedion be Governor in 2007? If free and fair elections are held, neither will be governor. The single most important factor that will determine who emerges is not elections but who ends up belonging to the PDP that is in control of Nigeria. The Esama has history on his side. He always ends up a friend of government. Chief Anenih is spending his last season in power. Given the fact that he is being weakened all round, it is most likely that by 2007, his influence will diminish to his local government area, or at best, his senatorial constituency. I have no sympathy for Chief Anenih because while he had power, he did not use it for the common good. He served the PDP to serve himself. One can remember that after declaring that there is no vacancy in Aso Rock, he went on to announce Chief Lucky Igbinedion as PDP candidate in Edo State, when the primaries had not been held. He enjoyed the attention in the press. He was described as the most powerful politician in Nigeria, the great Mr Fix it. Unfortunately, such people only get mention in history books where volumes and chapters are written about men and women who served well. There is a lesson to learn. That is that power is transient. We also live in an animal kingdom, where in the pride of power hungry people, the leader is devoured at the very first sign of weakness. Only foolish people will take sides in the current struggle within the PDP in Edo State. There is in fact no party, there are two people, i.e. Chief Anenih and Chief Igbinedion, and others are either their boys or slaves. If you ask me who will win, say the one who has the ground troops. Time is also running out for old men. In a decade, this era will be over. The old will die and the young will grow up.

Edo State people are suffering. There is no positive sign of development or improvement of the condition of the people. They are harassed in the streets by government thugs operating in the name of traffic agents. The powerful people in the state are the Agbero. They are the new business elite. The state is back again as a robber's haven. Every Edo indigene, except the police knows what is going on. The average Edo person has a big vision for life. So he or she "checks out". To make it big now, they can no longer travel. So they take to robbery because there are no jobs. The people are a proud people. In the past, it was impossible to find a beggar on the streets of Benin, even in the *SAP* days. There are beggars today. But if they are Edo people, they beg with style. Educated youth's mill around searching for good life. For them the Nigerian standard is inadequate. They will do anything to make it big. The other point is that the Agbero and cultists who were used for elections need to keep the high profile which their sponsors can no longer afford to provide. Besides those people once used as traffic enforcers lived on extortions and bribes. They are now used to big pay. Disbanding this group is one reason for the current robberies. We can understand the robberies; but why is there so much thirst for police blood?

I think powerful people are trying to send a statement that they are on ground. Petty robbers don't kill policemen. In fact, professional robbers wouldn't want to kill the police because it disrupts their business. The police killers in Edo State are political robbers; they are trying to make a point for themselves or for some people.

20 February, 2005

CHAPTER EIGHT

NATIONAL CON-FAB

I have a certain problem. When I hear a name, it evokes an image in my mind. This is not exactly like the condition known as synaesthesia. The latter occurs as a result of the linkage of sensory organs. A person hears a particular music and feels a sweet, bitter or tingling taste in his/her mouth. He or she may read certain letters and hear music of different sensation. Imagine walking in the street of Lagos and seeing diverse colours from hearing different sounds. I am not synesthetic. I think that what I am about to explain has not yet been named. Imagine for instance, that whenever I hear the name *PRONACO*, I always inexplicably think of one of those dubious construction companies or even a biscuit factory. The word *Wabara* makes me think of *waɛ̰kaɟ* in Hausa even though there is no logical connection. *Mantu*, I associate with a cattle specie *muturu*. For similar reasons, I think of *Masari* as a Kenyan of *Masai* decent. I believe that my problem is that I have spent too many years studying ideophones. Most words have a non-arbitrary relationship between sound and meaning but not so for ideophones. I am a freak of sort and you must pardon me if you introduce yourself and I appear to be scanning your name for associated images. To talk of a *Confab* leaves me with a sense of con men fabricating lies. A national Conference cannot be more than an attempt to nationalize inferences of some conmen. I wonder if anyone has done the arithmetic of the average age of those at the Confab. Oh! to call it a conference of Political reforms is even worse because, given what we know about politics and reform in Nigeria, we expect that at the end of the day, a new political party will emerge that will form the basis of the fifth republic which will start from 2007. Let us go back to the question of age of the *Confabulators*.

I think we have run out of people, especially young people in Nigeria. We seem also to be short of women. If the government was really after maturity, it may have paid us better to ask *Chief Imoudu* to chair the Confab, *Enahoro* or Venerable *Alayande* could be Secretary. As things are, one is afraid that many of the invitees are being paid to sleep in Abuja. Even if one could argue that age is not a factor in the selection process looking at the list, one recognizes a lot of notorious people. It would appear that notoriety is the primary criterion used by State Governments in the selection process. The other criterion appears to be that such a person be a spent force. In spite of all these, the Confab may yet produce good results. At least we expect no agreements to be reached. If the participants agree, it will be bad news for Nigeria because we will end up with a new party which will most likely succeed PDP. Take a look at history. Every such conference has always produced the new crew of leaders of our country. Each time people gather together for a national purpose like this, the main fruit has always been the birth of a new political association.

President Obasanjo's speech at the opening ceremony was unfortunately uninspiring. The kind of speech that should open such a gathering ought to be one that will move stones and pull down the pillars of scepticism. His speech lacked philosophy; it was poor in politics and lacking in emotions. I think the President is overwhelmed. One is afraid that even he has lost faith in the Confab. A leader must inspire leadership; he or she needs to demonstrate faith and purpose. His life must be an example of what he lays claim to. I think the President is just plodding on. I believe we need a conference. The President is right in seeking political reforms. But he is wrong again in playing God. Why is Federal Character, Presidentialism, Re-structuring, etc. no go areas? If these are at the heart of our political crises, why can't we talk about them? The President reminds me of the story of a man who was asked to adjudicate between a man and his wife and he declared that sex was not to be talked about. A few days later, he was called again to settle the same problems to his amazement. He will go back over and over until he is ready to listen to this very knotty matter. How can you settle a dispute between two Igbo if you do not want to discuss money? How possible is it to adjudicate between two Yoruba men if you would not ask about the woman in their lives? Can one possibly resolve a dispute between two Hausa males if one ignores power play?

I wish those who have gathered in Abuja to discuss our future happy holidays. There are beautiful places to visit like the Millennium Park. Make time to see those places.

While all the discussions are going on, they should remember that the Oputa Panel report is still being expected. There are numerous white papers from Government, which Nigerians are waiting for. If we do get this one out; it will mean that the communiqué of the conference was written long ago only awaiting signatures from so-called eminent Nigerians to legitimize it.

27 February, 2005

CHAPTER NINE

THE DOMINOS ARE FALLING

On 22 March 2005, the fight against corruption took on a new turn. After the fall of *Tafa*, no one thought we will be in this spectacle for a while. Mr President has sent the strongest signal ever. I am for the first time happy with him. I enjoyed every bit of his broadcast and in fact, I could have hugged him on the screen.

You need to see what happens when some of these minister's daughters are wedding. Heads of parastatals, Rectors and Vice Chancellors go to such weddings with gifts in sacks of currency. These people control their councils by bribing officials silly. Bribes are characteristically paid on government cheques and huge sums paid out as *PR*. Most of those successful people you see around in those expensive cars are really petty thieves. You see them on TV celebrating phantom success from loots. Do not envy them. The Pandora box has been opened and we should cooperate with the president. I would like to see something done about those Rectors and Vice Chancellors who habitually bribe visitation teams and waste the resources of their institutions on corrupt councils. As things are going no one will be safe from Ribadu. He is my man. Nigerians should write petitions to EFCC and supply them with facts. Someday, Obasanjo himself may have to answer some questions.

CHAPTER TEN

VANITIES UPON VANITIES

There is foolishness in the air and the sons of men have no remembrance of the words of Sages neither do they have remembrance of the lessons of life and nature. There is folly in the food we eat and idiocy in the water we drink so there is no balance in judgment and restraint in actions. I have communed with my own heart and searched for all the great men and women of means in our land, the very richest and greatest among them and I have seen all the works that they have done under the sun; behold, all is vanity and a vexation of the spirit. These people whose praises were sung by musicians, those who built churches and mosques, whose favour kings sought, I ask for them but none was found. All are gone with the wind. Moth and rust have destroyed their earthly treasures, and their remembrance is no more. Their treasures were on earthly things, their castles were built with hay, and they laid foundations on sand. The eternal thief has stolen their wealth; the moth and rust have overcome their treasures.

Time, the ultimate storm has blown away their castles. What profit hath a man for all his labour which he taketh under the sun? Our tears may flow like a river in expression of love for the dead; we may bury in caskets of gold and dress up the dead in apparels of silver, but these do not make up for a wasted life, a life of no real value. A life invested in vanities is vanities, no matter the eulogies of Priests, or the tears of relatives. A life spent in the pursuit of material things is lost no matter the recommendation of kings or the honours of men or the attendance at a burial. Dead men cannot give life to the dead. The dead may only bury their dead. Those who gather to feast at the burials of "great men" of vanities are themselves dead men waiting to die.

It is good to be at the burial of the great and watch the pomp and the display. Know that it is a drama put up by men and women who lacked courage to free themselves from the rule and reign of the flesh. Caskets of gold for the ground, apparels of silver for termites, buckets of tears to wash the iniquities; barrels of wine and legions of wine, fowls and cattle slain and consumed by those who were starved and deprived by the dead.

One last restitution before hell's gates are opened. Birthdays are celebrated as if dates of birth are in dispute. Titles are piled up to make up for the emptiness of life; buildings about like birds would build nest from season to season. Money stolen and stored up, like ants and termites. An unfulfilled and empty life cannot be compensated for by money or titles. Powerful men, rich men, death takes them away and there is no remembrance of them. I speak to you who are waiting to die and I say, you will surely die and naked and vulnerable, you will be in your grave. Listen to the darkness and let it speak to you. Hear the confessions of the wind and take it to heart; you are nothing, you are naked, you will surely die! Run your mind through time to thousands of years and see those who are remembered. How many of them are remembered by their wealth? Jesus? Buddha? Mohammed? Gandhi? Mother Theresa?

Those rich who are remembered are because they have left their wealth in public trust. You fool! Steal! Steal more! Pile up wealth for your generations! Sell Nigeria for your great grandchildren! The fate of fools surely will befall you because your generation cannot hold on to that which is not theirs and you surely will in hell have the reward for your folly. "... wise men die, likewise the fool and others. Their in-ward thought is, that their houses shall continue forever, and their dwelling places to all generations; they call their lands after their own names. Streets and schools; airports and barracks are named in their remembrance. They are preserved in graves to give men time to worship their remains and books of lies are written by the best liars to cover up their iniquities. This their way is their folly. Like shell they are laid in the grave; death shall feed on them; and the upright shall have dominion over them in the morning; and their beauty shall consume in the grave from their dwelling ... Be not afraid when one is made rich, when the glory of his house is increased; for when he dieth he shall carry nothing away; his glory shall not descend after him ... man that is in honour and understandeth not, is like the beasts that perish" (Psalm 49).

I cannot believe how fast a man can fall in life. Just a few weeks ago, Professor Okebukola was spitting fire in one of the newspapers. He threatened to sack corrupt lecturers automatically – perhaps by simply pressing the delete button on his word processor. Power is worse than wine. The man is now in trouble and he seems to be having difficulties talking his way out of it. When he lied with those cranked up evidence that he gave a loan to the minister of education in respect of Suleja Academy for an emergency, I knew that this was just a case of the proverbial tortoise that is bound to entrap himself. There was an emergency alright; just that it was very far from Suleja Academy. If there was a case of an outbreak of an epidemic, it was not reported. No case of fire outbreak or collapsed structures were reported either. It is now clear that the *ES* told a lie. He was part of the meeting and knew exactly what the money was all about and he obliged *Oga*. Do I blame him for that? Do you think I find him guilty of a cover up of all the balderdash about management meeting approving blah blah blah. It is like the case of the mad man who set the village on fire and when he was accused, he said that he only set fire to the rubbish heap, but that he is not responsible for the fire that devoured the whole village. As for *Osuji*'s attempt to distinguish between bribe and welfare, one is reminded of the leper who spat on the Mortar. When he was reprimanded, he removed the rag with which he dressed his wound and used it to clean the spittle. These professors are poor liars. *FUTO V.C.* is a tragic liar. Who else but a professor will take a whole ministry in tow to deliver a bribe and then reward the burden bearer with a handsome million? This is called academic bribery. Others did theirs quietly and are today presiding over their judgment at the Federal Executive Council. I think Osuji and Co. should take consolation that this is an act of God and they should accept their conviction, when it comes, in the interest of democracy and national development.

CHAPTER ELEVEN

OBJ'S ALLERGY

There have been speculations regarding why Obasanjo is suddenly allergic to corruption. Some think that he is trying to get at credible presidential materials for 2007. The reason is that he is interested in a third term. Well I can't see any credible contestant yet for 2007. It will be foolish for Mr. President to try a third time. One of those interested in Aso Rock I understand made his money from writing a book. Yeye dey smell. If it is that simple, University of Ibadan will be full of billionaires. The other more interesting suggestion is that Obasanjo has a terminal illness and he wants to do something he will be remembered for. I pray that whatever that illness is, it should get worse; but it should not kill him soon to allow him clean up this augean stable.

There is now fear in the land. As people search themselves to see how corrupt they have been. They are wondering if someday they will be called to account for their sins. Who no know go know. By the way, have you noticed that *Fabian Osuji* and *Osomo* have some physical resemblance? I hope Obasanjo has no special hatred for black and broad nosed ministers. I suggest others should consider adjusting their nose. I recommend a contract for nose adjustment. Put additional ten percent as welfare for the relevant house committee. Congratulations to the new ministers.

I suggest that their welfare packages to legislators to facilitate easy screening should be done through contracts and contractors. Communication of figures related to this should be in codes and sign language.

CHAPTER TWELVE

THE PAST: 1995

Reflecting on Nigeria, especially in the past few years, I have become increasingly aware of new, strong and emerging philosophies. A new code of conduct exists for Nigerians. If anything, Nigeria is a very exciting place to live in, in spite of the criticisms of our detractors in South Africa and the United Nations and disquieted elements in the United States and the Commonwealth, Nigeria is the most exciting place on (h)earth to live in.

I believe in Nigeria, I believe in our Government under the able leadership of General Sani Abacha (Long live the deity) and his team of highly patriotic and principled Nigerians.

I want to thank specially the information minister Quadruple Chief Walter Ofonagoro for his competence in the Business of Information Engineering and Management. One is not surprised that he has been duly recognized by the international community through several chieftaincy titles.

Nigeria is blessed with *rulers* and they are to be found in all *stakes* of the *nation*. Last time one of these *Nobull* Nigerians arrived from *Arsehole* rock singing the praises of the Government. I was very impressed by the level of his reasoning. He convinced me that *Ken Saro Wiwa* deserved what he got. He asserted that the *Ogoni* problem could not be solved in any other way. He expressed deep confidence in the *Lead Ass* of Nigeria. He praised the *Commander in Thief*, the *Con-minders*, the various *Gore-vernors, Con-missioners, Meaneaters*, *Vice-Chancellors*, etc. What impressed me most was his insistence that the rest of the world should leave Nigeria alone to solve her problems. In his opinion, the only solution to Nigeria's problem is for Nigeria to change the focus of her FOREIGN policy from Africa to Asia. He expressed sadness at the ingratitude of African Countries to Nigeria.

As far as he was concerned, countries like South Africa, Zimbabwe, Namibia, Liberia should support Nigeria at all times in every way. He criticized Mandela for his stand against Nigeria. He described him as an ingrate and greedy man. He argued that Nigerian *Polytricktians,* and *Profanessors* can handle Nigeria's problems. Ofonagoro stated that Mandela had asked Nigeria for $10m settlement several months before the Ogoni saga, but that General Abacha chided him for trying to corrupt him. In his usual benevolence, however, Abacha offered Mandela $.2m towards his second marriage. Mandela rejected this because it was too small.

Elder Wole Oyelese has been too much of a prayer warrior. He has risen to the challenges of the times. One must commend him for his spirituality and Christian discipline. He has carried his prayer campaign to every church in the land preaching the good news and making known to Nigerians their Saviour General Abacha. Elder Wole Oyelese has scored highly spiritually; he deserves to sit with the Pharisees and Sadducees.

The principle of dialogue has taken hold of the Nigerian Psyche. I have personally been taught that dialogue is an alarm which one should raise after dealing a hard blow to one's opponent. The man who holds the power does not and cannot dialogue – it is the aggrieved who should. Violence took on a new meaning. Non-violent agitation is to go to Aso Rock with a solidarity message. If you write any article against government you are violent. 1995 was a year of solidarity rallies and visits. It was a year of rented crowds. That was a year when the best business was the rental one-rent-a- crowd. I dare to say that no government in the history of Nigeria has enjoyed as much support as the Abacha government. From all states of the federation, people poured into Abuja to *suppress support* to the government. I was amazed that so many Nigerians were so zealous with patriotic zeal at such times.

What worried me though was that the government appeared insensitive to the solidarity visits. With so much support one became confused that government was bothered by the negative reports from the newspapers. Government appeared not to be aware of the huge support they have as showed by the solidarity visits.

They persisted in asking for support from the same people who have so willingly visited Aso Rock with solidary messages. The visitors themselves appeared almost always uninterested in their message once in Abuja. They were often seen fighting, quarrelling and shouting over some items of gratitude from government.

15 May, 2005

CHAPTER THIRTEEN

THE OBASANJO LIBRARY

The quickest way to ruin your image in Nigeria is to speak in support of President Obasanjo. The man vacillates like a gnat. Today, he is a raging inferno against corruption, tomorrow he is actively promoting it. One is really shocked that while Mr President is fighting to reduce the cost of praise-singing in the newspapers, he would permit such a huge sum of money to be spent stroking his ego. Our leaders are just something else.

There are so many immoral things going on in this government that is shouting itself hoarse about transparency and accountability. It is bad enough that members of this government have used their positions to obtain licenses for private Universities and are now hell-bent on privatizing public Universities. It is worse that while they are under funding these same universities, they permit public funds to be committed to white elephant ego pandering monuments to Mr President. ₦7b is enough to make the libraries of the first generation Universities top end. But who would think of these Universities since the libraries will not be named after Mr President. I have been to many trainings on how to raise funds for Universities and I have always tried to let people understand that you do not get money in Nigeria because you have beautiful ideas, inventions or well-articulated proposal. If you are not worshipping a prominent Nigerian or his late father, you get nothing. That is why Universities now habitually sell doctoral degrees to people who are best locked up in cells of ignorance.

The other way to raise funds is to get these same people on campuses to give worthless talks for thirty minutes and spend the better part of two hours cajoling them with imaginary achievements. I have no problems with individuals donating to the president's library so that they can continue to get contracts. It is however absolutely corrupt for government parastatals to commit public money to such projects.

Even donations made by private individuals are hardly voluntary when you come to think of it. People grumble and complain that they feel pressured into making these donations. Many see it as investment which they must recoup. I have heard it suggested that about two hours after the library fund was launched, the price of rice and cement went up. There is something called abuse of office. This is a clear case of it. It is the elder sister to corrupt enrichment. I hope that someday, someone will conduct a study on how much of public fund is committed to praise singing and servicing the ego of the leaders of this country. From the anniversaries, the birthdays celebrated at odd years and numerous programmes of first ladies, to burial ceremonies and weddings, the figure must be in billions. It will be nice for someone to evaluate the projects of the first ladies to determine in an objective sense if they are really worth it.

CHAPTER FOURTEEN

WILL NIGERIA DISINTEGRATE?

A few days ago, the American Government was in the news in Nigeria. It was all about the claim that Nigeria is likely to break up at some point. I was amazed that this made news because, for over ten years now, Nigeria has been on the risk list as a country with a high potential for disintegration.

I do not think that Nigeria will break up because the American government says it will but I think it will be foolish to dismiss this opinion simply because it was first expressed ten years ago and it has not come to pass. I think it calls for sober reflection. Mr President should not simply dismiss the statement after all, he is a mere man.

He may have succeeded in holding Nigeria together today by force of politics but what will happen when he leaves the stage?

As a matter of fact, has Nigeria not disintegrated already? Do we really have a country? I think honestly that Nigeria broke up years ago, and we are only now trying to put it to back together. The American government arrives at its conclusions through intelligence work and by research – measuring all kinds of indicators. The indicators are really bad for Nigeria. The conflicts and ethnic tension, social inequalities, corruption, assassination, general discontent, murders, strife and disrespect for law and order all point to a nation in disarray. The reason this country has not gone the natural way of war is simply because it will not be in the interest of the West to have war in Nigeria.

The state of our economy and our level of technology is such that we cannot by ourselves sustain modern warfare without external cooperation. International politics and oil politics as it stands today is in favour of maintaining a Nigerian Nation even with all its contradictions. Consequently, even the most hot-headed Nigerian will have enormous problems obtaining support for war from the West. We must also be grateful for the fall of the Soviet bloc. The ideological polarization which could easily have formed the basis for justifying support for conflict is no more there. The world now moves in one direction and America is the Engine while Europe is the carriage. The rest of us are passengers. The Nigerian politician himself knows no ideology except money. He has absolutely no convictions and feels strong about nothing but profit. What will push him to war if he continues to make money? The common man cannot make war. He can only revolt. Even in revolt, he is a simply a tool in the hands of the elite who has enough means to finance such a revolt. There are no such elites in Nigeria. Life is too sweet and too pleasurable to the Nigerian elite such that dying is not an option at all.

We must first of all thank the West that we are not in disarray. As long as our leaders continue to play the good boy and use the right terminologies, we will not disintegrate. Why should the West care much about progress in Nigerian today? Why must they create another China in Africa and ruin their own comfort mortally? We are like a sick person who should be kept alive at all cost but must not be allowed to get well. There are two scenarios that could spell great potentials for disintegration for Nigeria. The first is if president Obasanjo decides to run for a third term. The second is, if substantial quantities of oil are struck in Northern Nigeria. Nigeria will disintegrate only if Northern Nigeria feels unable to continue to be part of the Nigerian assemblage. It is easy to see how religion could be used to make an argument for secession. It is also easy to see how such a project could be financed.

The South-South leaders will never be able to sufficiently muster enough forces to compromise Nigeria's integrity. It will continue to be an irritation. Truth is, the current revolt is largely a proletarian revolt with perhaps surreptitious support from some elites. For the elite, the revolt constitutes a platform for negotiating advantage in the Nigerian equation. You could see that the political elite in the South-South do not care about the exploitation of their people neither do they care about pollution and deprivations. Name any politician of substance who has taken up the struggle except on the pages of newspapers. Who of them has come out openly to organize a peaceful revolt? What I see though are plunderers, people who dredge streams and rivulets and open up factories that produce imaginary goods. I see people whose identity cannot be ascertained; grand patrons of bunkerers. For many elite, the agitation for resource control is an instrument for relevance and there is no visible commitment to the struggle than the fight to create dynasties.

Neither the Yoruba nor Igbo will go to war. If none of the major ethnic groups go to war, then there will be no war. Minorities are now very familiar with the implications of revolt. The crushing of Odi, the routing of Tiv communities has taught minorities to bear their troubles with courage. The majority groups will not war because mass poverty has kept the common man occupied with issues of daily living. He does not see his redemption coming from streets but from the sky. Truth is that people don't fight when they can still find hope. There is an abundance of hope in Nigeria. Nigerians go to mosques every Friday to recharge their hope batteries. Each time they have enough power to last the week and in fact some to spare their neighbours who remain at home. We are too religious to fight. The point is that faith may justify war but only when such faith puts the group above the individual. In our situation, the group matters only as a platform for personal redemption. The group has no real value if it cannot produce the tangible material benefits. Suffering has failed to change our orientation? With so much suffering, with so much spite and oppression from our leadership, it is a marvel that our people still assemble to celebrate the killers of their children.

Will such a people ever fight? NO! There will be no war. Never! The suffering continues. Unless we emancipate ourselves from mental slavery, we will never sing the redemption song

CHAPTER FIFTEEN

BEGGING FOR FORGIVENESS

Nothing is more revealing of our moral corruption than our willingness to forgive sins that were not committed against us in the first instance. After, every crisis, it is typical to hear people calling for reconciliation, and forgiveness. A typical example is the Jos crisis. There was so much to talk about reconciliation that one felt that the term had been abused and used as a reason to avoid justice and doing the right thing. The issue remains whether what led to the crisis has been dealt with. If people breached the law have they been dealt with, or are the laws of the land open to reconciliation? Is the law no more an ass? *Dariye* has returned, in spite of everything, a hero of sort.

Now, people have asked him to forgive his so called enemies. Of course, his supporters do not believe in forgiveness. We so much personalize the apparatus of state to the point that we forgive sins committed against the state simply because we happen to be in a position of authority. How do we forgive a murderer if we cannot recall the dead? In Rivers State, one has heard that Mr President has graciously forgiven and granted unconditional pardon to the gangs. In fact, they have been praised for accepting the forgiveness. So what will happen to innocent people who were killed in these gang wars! Too many people are above the law in our country that is why we will never have a country. Begging is part of our political culture. And I have a feeling that our leaders ask to be begged just as they hire crowds to praise them. Every disagreement leads to a begging parade. We have become so adept at this to the extent that traditional rulers are often drafted to provide the mats on which beggars lie.

CHAPTER SIXTEEN

RESOURCE CONTROL

I just got called to be the President of Nigeria in 2007. In fact, I dreamt that Obasanjo handed over to me amidst great pomp and pageantry. Even in the dream, I was puzzled and confused because I am not a member of the PDP. I am also not from Northern Nigeria. I dream a lot and hear a lot of voices calling me to do many things. But I am honest enough with myself to realize that God has nothing to do with most of what I hear and dream about. One thing I must confess to you is that I am not holy enough to get a telephone call from God. One reason I often discard my dream is that I dream most when I am broke and when I am about to have malaria. So you can imagine that as soon as I wake up, I go for malaria prophylactic.

There are many holy men of God who wait for God to tell them to rise from their beds in the morning before they do so. They have become so holy that they ask him how many wraps of Amala they should eat.

Sometimes, common people like me get inspired to seek office; we do not ascribe this to God. Sometimes, it is others who encourage us to seek for office. At other times, we simply are covetous or greedy of gain and we encourage people to encourage us or pay others to inspire us. Holy men are above this meanness. God speaks to them through GSM lines.

Prof. Obaje, the President of all chaplains is one holy man who has been called to serve in a lower office as the Governor of Kogi State. If he does that, he will only be like so many legislators in my State who left the State Assembly to become Chairmen of Local Government Areas. Some Commissioners have also become Personal Assistant to Ministers. Unlike Obaje, these people have confessed to some people in private that they are doing it for the money. Assemblymen don't control any meaningful budget. Our most distinguished reverend stated clearly that the office of the Governor of Kogi is beneath him having held so many distinguished positions. Even as I write, you probably don't know that I am the First Black man to dream of having a white man as a house help. My name should be in the Guinness Book of Records for this. Do you know in fact that some people have corrupted Obaje's name without really meaning to do so, to mean "an indulgent person". If you pronounce the name with a sub dot under the first and last letters, with the right tonal combination in Yoruba, that is exactly what it will mean. You can work it out.

Some of us are so plain holy, that when our own greed and covetousness is propelling us we think that we are hearing from divinities. I think the honourable reverend is simply trying to join the race for resource control at the micro level. One can control the resources of a State for the good of himself and his household, his village or his ethnic group. The whole problem of corruption, tribalism, nepotism, rotational Presidency, etc. is all about resource control or its extreme version of resource commandeering. Let us take the simple case of political positions. In Oyo State, if you are a chicken and you are from Ibadan, you can become Governor. No matter who you think you are, if you are not a son of the soil, the best you can hope for is to be a balancing stool for the Ibadan man. In Edo State, a Benin goat will be Governor over an Archangel from elsewhere. The other ethnic groups in Kogi are the rags, which the Igala employ to clean their shoes. Take the Tiv in Benue or Urhobo in Delta. In the Local government areas, the story is not different. It is a classic tale of bigger groups bulling smaller ones in order to corner national resources. As we go up to the Centre, the stakes get higher. It was once the Hausa-Fulani using Yoruba and Igbo as balancing legs in a tripod stool. One of the legs threatened to break and so, it was allowed to control power from under. The eyes of the Niger Delta peoples have opened and they know that crude oil is sweet. They also now want to control resources as the fourth leg of a stool that will develop more legs in the future if we do not stop this foolishness and primitive instinct that is threatening us as a people. The problem of resource control also rears its head in our Universities by way of the ethnicisation of the office of the Vice Chancellor. Another dimension of this is the demand for local content in the appointment. In some Universities, people from other Universities are screened out or simply advised not to apply. This is a very foolish thing to do in an era when more serious people go all over the world to seek for the best candidates to occupy the office. The perception of universities as financial resource bases has led to the struggle to control the resources by contending forces. Resource control is also an issue when some traditional rulers refuse to accept rotation of the chair of traditional councils.

I would not like to think that I am trivializing the issue of resource control. What I am trying to say is that whether we call it corruption, tribalism, nepotism, domination, etc., we are simply giving many names to one evil called oppression or domination. Characteristically, we think that the solution is to rotate positions or opportunities so that different groups can take turns in oppressing their fellows. My case in Nigeria, as a minority is hopeless. Born in a family of nine, I am in a minority by my ideas. In my local Government area, as an Emai, I am a minority. Even though the headquarters is in my village, other groups sit as chairmen over the Local Government Area. My senatorial district is a minority in the State, so also is my State a minority in Nigeria. So, you can understand why my dream of taking over from Obasanjo in 2007 had to become a malaria induced Nightmare. How can that possibly happen given whom I am and who I have become by the grace of Nigeria. Socially speaking, I am neither related to any traditional ruler nor associated with any political heritage. My father died a poor man and in spite of what I have attained by divine providence, I am not a factor in local issues.

Then, why must I dream? You see, we are a nation besieged by folly; we are in competition to gain error.

There are no old and wise people in our land. There cannot be. We are simply in a market place; we trade every five days, disperse to reassemble in the next market day. The depths to which we have fallen are typified by the fall of holy men to the low estate of carnality. Yesterday, it was Okotie who got the call. A young man perhaps called by his zeal and good intentions for Nigeria. He probably misunderstood inspiration for the voice of God. But when the old and revered say they heard a shout from God; what then will become of men and women who need them to get up from their graves? God save us from our flesh!

3 July, 2005

CHAPTER SEVENTEEN

DEBT RELIEF

I would like to propose that an annual holiday be instituted to celebrate the debt relief or forgiveness given to Nigeria. This holiday can be flagged off with a Usury Sunday or a Zakat Friday. Why not? The sense of accomplishment and relief that followed this great *Oyibo* magnanimity makes it necessary for us to set aside a day to celebrate the Oyibo for their large heartedness. After all, after God, we have the Oyibo. There are in fact some who believe that if you meet an Oyibo on the way to Church or if you meet a Saudi on the way to the Mosque you should go back home because you have already encountered God. We need a statue of Tony Blair in Abuja. Rural Nigerians should be encouraged to make an annual pilgrimage to the statue in appreciation for the forgiveness of their sins of indebtedness. I am told that our beloved finance minister, Dr Iweala shed tears of joy when she heard that our sins have been forgiven. In fact, we understand that she has the *Sam Mbakwe Syndrome*. Each time negotiations involving Nigeria gets tough, she is said to sob. How dearly she loves her fatherland! She is a rare kind of patriot to be so emotional about her country. Well, I think she can take consolation in the hard currency she earns as salary. Dollars may sometimes evoke strong emotions that may be mistaken for patriotism.

There is no doubt that Mr President's numerous journeys are beginning to payoff. He was the one who started the business of borrowing in Nigeria. He opened our eyes to the forbidden apple. Now he is showing us the way out of usury. I don't know if it was a sense of relief or pardon or achievement that propelled Mr President into making a national broadcast. Whatever it was, he obviously felt that having our debts relieved is a monumental achievement. Actually, I agree with him. After all, our ancestors once celebrated when they signed off their sovereignty for sugar, mirrors and tobacco. The Oyibo man always thinks ahead of us. Talk to a moneylender if you know one and he will tell you that debts are never forgiven but they may be collected indirectly if you are sure that your debtor is terminally ill. However, as part of an image laundry, for other reasons a money lender may forget your debt because he has already squeezed his juice out and will like to make some moral capital for his bad image.

Nigeria's debt relief is stinking with hypocrisy. First, why was our entire debt not written off? Simple! They had their eyes on our swelling foreign reserves. If they really meant to help Nigeria, they should have forgotten what was left to be paid. The amount which we need to pay back is a clever way of getting back profits we made from higher price of gasoline.

The Paris Club of money lenders and their members thrive in usury. Rather than giving us debt relief, they ought to apologize to the ordinary Nigerian for years of slavery. The real problem of Africa is that there is a safe haven in the west for stolen money.

If our leaders steal and even as much as put some of it to work in the local economy, we will witness some levels of economic development. Even if they are not interested in the people for reasons of their loot, they will seek to create the right environment for productivity even when they are out of power. Many western nations were transformed by bootleggers and gangsters. Our case is different in the sense that stolen money does not stay in the house.

We have a severe problem with capital flight. Given the current global environment, it will not be long before we get into debt again. What we need is a just and fair global environment. The criminal insistence on the removal of subsidies and termination of social spending so readily accepted by our highly trained experts cannot be justified in the face of huge subsidies on Agriculture in Europe and America. We are actually the ones subsidizing the excessive taste for leisure and exaggerated incomes in the west. The amount of subsidy on a European cow is enough to fly it round the world twice in first class. Nigerian cows now want to check out. Unfortunately, the first group got killed by Air France at the Port Harcourt Airport.

I think the biggest problem we are facing is the burden of a deluded elite who too often go into elaborate day dreaming when the Oyibo humour's them with compliments about their intellect. African Presidents hang pictures of themselves shaking hands with Oyibo half their age in their villas. It is pitiable to see them standing like waiters or humanized ducks behind G8 presidents and feeling so exalted and accomplished at invitations to wait tables. A few words of infantile encouragements, humiliating pat on bald pates and they rush to press conferences to celebrate.

Why should one be impressed that President Bush calls Obasanjo his friend! A leader or an elite without ideology or clear cultural paradigms for social and political development is worse than an enemy soldier. Of what use is a slave with a PhD? Who is the greater slave? The man who is an ordinary slave or one who occupies the office of a Chief Slave? Obviously, there are very brilliant and cerebral individuals in the corridors of power. There are highly accomplished Africans all over the world. But of what use is a genius without common sense or native wisdom? Such a person is not better than a spy.

CHAPTER EIGHTEEN

TRUTH WEARS NO DISGUISE

I would like to congratulate University of Ilorin 44 for their victory in the court of law. Justice may be long in coming but it surely comes. Falsehood may triumph a hundred years but it surely fails. The University has gone ahead again without the knowledge of Council to appeal the judgement. The fall at the appeal court will only be greater. The University of Ilorin stinks.

Let me also encourage the Lagos State Government to persevere. One must not surrender principles to expediency. We cannot have greater trials in this land than we had under Abacha. We are still here and Abacha is no more. Long after the powerful rulers of today are gone we will still be here. Those who fail to listen to the courts will not have the courts in their time of need. People will be tried in this country whether they like it or not. We shall see.

7 August, 2005

CHAPTER NINETEEN

SUCCESSFUL CONFERENCE: UNSUCCESSFUL CRITICS

The National Political Reforms Conference has generated a new kind of debate in the newspapers. It was Matthew Hassan Kukah who started it all by blaming the press for focusing on negatives and in-consequential. At that point, I was under the impression that the press may have reneged on an agreement to portray the conference in positive light no matter what.

Mr President and his friends, as well as the conference leadership and "patriotic Nigerians" have all come out forcefully to emphasize that the *NPRC* was quite a successful assembly. According to Obasanjo, this is the most successful of such conferences so far in the history of Nigeria. What ignoble history to compare anything with. Mr President went further to lash out at his critics. As I read him and his executives each time I had a feeling that those who criticize him and his style may one day kill him with words. I wonder why he is ever so sensitive and quick to take every opportunity to say "shame to the devil". The Honourable Minister of Finance also had words for critics when Nigeria got debt relief. I think our leaders hear too much.

Justice Niki Tobi also came out to say that NPRC delegates agreed on 185 of 187 issues. This is elementary and trivial arithmetic. In his reasoning, in a democracy, the majority has its "bloody way" and the minority accepts its "sulky say". I think humanity has gone beyond this terrorism. The majority must recognize the rights of the minority in spite of number and minorities must respect the rule of law notwithstanding the logic of its argument. This is why compromise and collaboration are preferred to forcing as a strategy in negotiations. On resource control, what happened was clearly a dialogue of infants. The technical competence of the leadership of the conference showed a clear deficit.

I think an agreement could have been reached. If an agreement could not be reached on an explosive and decisive issue like resource control, one can hardly conclude that the conference was successful. If it was so successful, why did the South-South stay away from the President's reception?

I think that the South-South should have accepted a 17% and an increase to 25% over five years. There is a difference between what is ideal and what is realistic. Ideally, one would like to see an immediate jump to 50% but the consequences of this on other states of the federation will not be to the good of anyone including the South-South. The other point is that an injustice of a hundred years cannot be corrected overnight.

It was particularly unfair for Northern delegates to insinuate that the South-South have been misusing and embezzling budgetary allocations. It is quite true that a lot of money has been allocated to this region in the last few years. But the North is hardly free from corruption. What did the North do with derivation funds under the regional arrangement? It is easy to see how the West used its own funds. Even today, governments, especially local governments typically share resources among a few people. The problem of corruption is national and we must all brace up to address it. I think a more sober outlook would have suggested a more conciliatory approach by other zones. The stance of the North was to justify oppression on the grounds that more people are happy with the arrangement. What we all know is that if any of the major groups ever find oil in sufficient quantity, the story will be different.

I think the Northern Leadership ought to be ashamed that with the resources available to them in agriculture and solid minerals, they are fighting for hand-out from other regions. It is the share laziness, greed and misrule by those who are today pretending to be working for Northern interest that is responsible for the sorry state of the Northern masses. One feels sorry for the so-called South-South because they seem to have missed the whole point. More oil money will never develop the South-South. Oil will breed people like Asari; will produce gold-chain wearing youths, jeep driving middle class, and pot-bellied ill-mannered bowler hat politicians. But the Niger Delta will remain largely polluted and infested with poverty. Any wise government will invest in human capital. If not, no matter how much is ceded to the South-South. The money will seep into regions with requisite human resources. I think we need now carry out a study to find it out where current allocations go. I suspect that after the governors and their friends have taken a chunk, a good portion ends up in the pockets of indigenes of other zones who supply food, run taxis, provide specialized skills and run businesses. The youth in the South-South will continue to depend on extortion. They are either bush inspectors or inventing shrines to extort money.

What many Nigerians did not know is that it was self-interest and personal ambition that ruined the conference. Even the South-South was not together because of those who are interested in 2007. Delegates were simply playing election politics in the name of their people. Some regions said one thing in the papers and did another at the conference. 2007 will provide the South-South an opportunity to punish those who did not support them. But can they? There is no need to be discouraged. A lock vote against any presidential candidate will completely ruin such a candidate. But, truth is, there is no South-South – just a couple of vociferous hat-wearing and ambitious politicians.

The six-year single term for the President and Governors looked to me like a good proposal. But this was again ruined by politics and suspicion. The North wants two-terms in the next dispensation but are too blind to realize that they cannot have the presidency given the situation on ground. Except of course PDP again rigs it for them. It may not be so easy this time because some of the big riggers themselves have their special interests. There is some suspicion that Obasanjo wants to have the first shot at the single six-year term. For this reason the six-year term was opposed. The politicians are behaving like the proverbial pig who asked humans to stop defecating because she wants to stop eating faeces. She was told to stop complaining and ignore the faeces because man must shit. In reply she said a pig must be a pig; a pig must chop shit. Simple national solution to the President's so-called third term ambition is for our lawmakers and politician to ensure that appropriate legal instruments are used to block him. What one is hearing from them is that they will chop shit if the President is allowed to stoop. So the solution is to ensure that his anus is blocked. Again, man must shit!

Are there no ways of legally ensuring that the president is disqualified? Even if there are none, if the politicians really feel so strong about not having him back, he certainly will not make it. I think the fear is that they know that 'money for hand back na ground'.

14 August, 2005

CHAPTER TWENTY

KILLING FOR 2007

2007 is more than a full year away, yet the business of governance stopped almost a year ago when Governors started to declare their interest in contesting a second term. In Nigeria, typically, in a four year term, the first two-years are spent touring and saying thank you, getting used to terrorizing people with sirens and the pomp of office; delivering empty promises; attending parties and birthdays and delivering hollow speeches.

The second two years are spent seeking re-election. 2007 is beginning to look like the year of the gun! What we are experiencing now looks like a pack of dogs baring their teeth at one another.

We are taking the game of territoriality beyond what is normal. All over the country from Akwa Ibom to Ekiti, from Oyo to Edo, there is one problem or the other. People are being assassinated, deputies and speakers are being forced out of office and politicians are generally carrying on as if there is no life outside of politics.

The problem in Anambra, Edo and Oyo is simple. Godfathers have been disowned by their godsons and so the rest of the state have to pay. Two issues are always the matter: money and power. In no single case can one point to the people or programmes as the reason for this disagreement.

Shockingly too, there is nowhere we have political crisis in Nigeria where the ruling party, PDP is not either in power or struggling to wrest power. Lagos is being threatened with a PDP Tsunami. What a term to draft into politics. If the likes of Ogunlewe, Bode George and their Power Drunken People knew what a Tsunami is, they will not assault people's sensibilities by talking about Tsunami in Lagos. The only viable location of a Tsunami in 2007 is Abuja, if a third term option is implemented as being speculated.

27 August, 2005

CHAPTER TWENTY-ONE

CLEAR THE RING: OLUSEGUN THE BRUTE VERSUS MASKMAN ATIKU

At last, the President and his Vice are in the open arena of a village contest. What has been the subject of speculations for some time was finally confirmed by the President on T.V. live. I have never ceased to be fascinated by how easy it is to get Mr President to react. He is so plain easy to provoke to anger that one feels that there is need to do a psychological analysis of his childhood and background. How can a cocktail of a question lead to such deep response? Now that we are told that Mr Atiku is disloyal, what next? Will impeachment proceeding be instituted against him? Will he resign? No! In the weeks to come, we are going to see both men hugging for every silly reason and eating pounded yam together on T.V. The rest of us will be expected to applaud like mentally retarded people. Our country is a soap opera. Nobody wants to wake up from it even though the story is so drab, uninteresting and sickening.

Obasanjo and Atiku should never have been a pair. But that is what politics in Nigeria is all about. What can one expect from a country where lunatics control traffic? This is also a land where blind men teach Visual Arts and Village Farmers teach biotechnology. If sane people can be so insane behind wheels and it takes a madman to recognize their insanity, how sane then are we.

It is also in Nigeria that street urchins are employed as Security men and touts are consulted as opinion leaders. This is a nation of unusual people, senile old people who should be given special care in an old people's home are the great advisers and opinion leaders and worse still, unstable individuals are paraded as agents of god. Forgive me!

This is a diversion. Believe me or not, I respect Mr President. I also believe that he is as much a victim of our system as the rest of us. But can a man give what he does not have in himself?

The president and his Vice are very talented individuals who would have excelled against the British during the punitive expedition against the Benin Kingdom. There is absolutely no doubt that both men would make good kings in a kingdom. The world has left that era behind. One is shocked that the Presidency of the biggest black nation on earth has been reduced to a local wrestling brawl. That is what we are destined for as a people.

Nigerians should not be misled into believing that the disagreement between the duo has any foundation in principles or loyalty. The issue is 2007, succession, power, the Presidency. Obasanjo is interested in 2007 either by himself or through a surrogate. Atiku thinks that he ought to be the President but is not happy that Obasanjo is not delivering the mandate to his laps. Both men are wrong and are enemies of democracy. The people rightly determine who is President – not Obasanjo or Atiku.

Atiku seems also to have reached the conclusion that God and Nigerians don't want him as well. We all seem also to have concluded that Obasanjo and PDP will determine who becomes the next President. May we all live to see 2007. One has read that President Obasanjo is quite worried about who succeeds him. I think it is responsible of him to harbour worry. But to be paranoid about succession is something that he needs to avoid. I chuckle when I hear that he wants a successor who will carry on his reforms and good works. The Minister of Technology just informed us that the reforms would be on for twenty-five years. I hope that we all realize that these good works are incessant increase in cost of fuel, spiralling inflation, mass poverty and disease. A lot of the so-called reforms have produced positive results only in World Bank and IMF reports. As a layman, I have little understanding of economic theories and their logic. But I can tell you that in the last few years, we have had more of the same thing; I have witnessed lots of activities but little action;

lots of motion but no movement. Plenty of promises no tangibles. If what one is seeing in the land is progress, I want to be backward.

For me and many others, economics and development is all about slogans and propaganda. The only visible evidence of change we can see is in government officials and politicians who are building houses about like birds and buying properties in South Africa. They and their families and close associates have certainly made much progress. For those in government and those benefiting from the corrupt, unfair and unjust system, it is easy to say that there 'is progress. It is not so easy for the over 70% of Nigerians who live below poverty lines. Each time it appears as if Nigerians are beginning to get a handle on things, something is done to set them back a couple of years. Government officials and their relatives know nothing about what yam costs in the market. When they fall ill, they are flown abroad. Their children attend schools in Europe and America at public expense. We are called to make sacrifices. But that is all we have been doing. Some are in the habit of consuming our sacrifices like witches who cannot be appeased. We are running two countries in Nigeria. One is for the government and the other is for the people. Our experiences and realities are so different that it is impossible to get good governance.

Let me leave with this word. There is a difference between shopping for a successor and scheming for one. The only true way to shop for a successor is by free and fair elections. It is only by the will of the people that the right person can emerge. Real economic progress will come when Nigerians gain control of the instruments of power, when they can hire and fire their leaders. Economic progress cannot happen when people lack motivation; where there is a failure of will and mass discontent. Our primary problems are socio-political and psychological. The economic ones are consequence of these. The solution is the restoration of confidence; the rebirth of hope through enfranchisement: mobilization through popular participation; motivation through inspired leadership.

4 September, 2005

CHAPTER TWENTY-TWO

OGBEH'S NEMESIS

The newspapers are awash with claims by the former PDP Chairman Chief Audu Ogbeh of the threats to his life. Yesterday, the man was called a henchman, a power broker, a chieftain and he savoured every moment in power. If you want to know what happens to people when they are out of power and favour in Nigeria, talk to Ogbeh. This was a man who used to lick OBJ's behind when it was well between them. He came out to justify every silly action of government even before government could conjure an explanation. Now he is running scared about assassins and we are expected to come out with cudgels to protect him.

There is a very long list of people who were assassinated when Chief Ogbeh was Chairman of PDP. What did he do? If anything happens to him he will be one of many before him, some of whom are more eminent than he. The problem with the average Nigerian elite in a leadership position is that he forgets that power is transient.

Often we wear leadership like a cloak and treat government like a cartel. We are ever so overcome by power and blinded by office that we forget that we were nothing before we got into office. Nowhere in the world are politicians so puffy and disrespectful of the people as in Nigeria. No condition is permanent. Chief Ogbeh should hire his own *meguard* because that is what the rest of us do. Or better still, he should consult *Babalawos* to prepare charms against gunshots and cutlass for him that is what his colleagues do. If we fail to do something while we are in position to do it, we will have to live with the reality and consequences of our inaction. I hope Alli is also listening.

11 September, 2005

CHAPTER TWENTY-THREE

NEPOTISM

I read recently in the papers how the current PDP Chairman fixed up his wife and son. Our own eminent Tsunami Bode George tried to justify this as a norm. Something he himself would do of course. Nigerians are just being insulted by our so-called leaders. We are basically slaves in this country and the masters are in government.

The issue about Alli's conduct is not whether his wife and son are qualified but that he has taken advantage of his office for personal gain. This is Nepotism. Let us not stop at Alli because Alli's actions would not be remarkable if he were not Chairman of PDP.

The current political landscape is filled with this stench; for instance, Kwara State ought to be renamed Saraki land. Edo should be called Okada wonderland. Wherever people have gained political advantage in this country, they have used it to benefit generations unborn in their lineage. Appointments by Federal and State Governments is done in part by blood. Big time politicians and past military and civilian leaders have all been settled through appointments of their children and relations.

When they scream about discrimination or injustice it is because they want to be noticed. Run through the list of politicians of substance in the country and tell me whose family has not been settled. Our country is becoming more like a kingdom. My prayer is that our children will not end up serving their children as we and our fathers have served their fathers. There is a bigger headache beyond what Alli has done. This has to do with our employment practices. Many businesses and government establishments are paralyzed because of incompetent leadership and poor hiring practices.

We are all over the place screaming that the quality of graduates from Nigerian Universities has dropped. But have we ever considered the fact that even those who are qualified don't get appointed? Most of us find a way to bring in relatives, girlfriends and members of our sects into our establishments.For many, it is a religious duty to populate their establishment with their kinds. So what do we expect when we employ incompetent people! The practice of temporary appointment has been perfected as a way of loading places of work with undesirable elements. Worse than this is the fact that interviews are stage managed for predetermined individuals. Things have become so bad that applicants are even asked to draw up requirements for positions they are expected to compete for.

Many of us are guilty of filling up positions with incompetent individuals. Many are guilty of recommending for promotion those we know are ill prepared for certain responsibilities. We do this yet we complain and blame others for the problems in our nation. The incompetent doctors, corrupt politicians, murderous policemen and exploitative teachers all arise because we compromise the system when we should strengthen it. I am always amused when I listen to elderly people castigate and condemn the younger generation. But they never pause to reason about how this generation came to be what they are. Every generation lays the foundation for and nurtures the succeeding one. The good old days is a sign of failure of those who recount those days. It is a sign that they have failed to pass on the benefits they enjoyed to successive generations. The success or failure of any generation is largely dependent on the seeds of the previous one. So all the cry about falling standards, corruption, and lawlessness can be traced to the generation of those above the golden years. After all, even today, they are the ones ruling; formulating policies and discharging all kinds of wickedness. They are the fathers and mothers of those they currently castigate. If their children have failed, isn't it because they have been poor parents? They may blame their own parents for their own failures, but they must take responsibility for the emerging tendencies and failures. They obviously have failed their children. In the Universities, Professors talk about the standards while they were in school as if they created those standards. They go on to deride younger colleagues as incompetent and interlopers as if they are not the ones who taught them and hired them. They talk about the collapse of discipline but forget to mention their roles as agents in the process. Each one of those so called super Academic today enjoyed government's lavish support towards training and international exposures. They got refined through deliberate grooming by serious people before them who understood the basis of development. Today all we have are screamers.

People are so busy trying to make geniuses out of themselves because they now have a generation of academics who have become so localized that they cannot even recognize their own image. Among some of the most ardent critics of standards are those who should be lashed with canes for failing to mentor younger academics. There are not many today who can point to even two academics who they mentored in the course of thirty years. Look at the list of Ph.D. produced and see what I mean. Talk to their students and you will be shocked by what they think of them.If we produce substandard Ph.Ds. and proceed to employ and promote such individuals over better qualified individuals, do we have any right to complain? I am of the opinion that our nation's resources was spent on a generation who consumed everything like caterpillars and left nothing for their own children. They are also the ones screaming today that their children have all gone bad.

18 September, 2005

CHAPTER TWENTY-FOUR

CORRUPTION

My daughter sometimes gets a spanking for being naughty. Most times, I reprimand her and try to get her to understand why she is being reprimanded. It is a tiring exercise because one has to repeat the same thing over and over and over. The easier approach is to instill fear into her by warming her buttocks. Of course, I use the rod, but sparingly. She gets a hard treatment whenever she does wrong and tries to drag in her brother as an accomplice. I don't often mind her pleading innocence and arguing her way out of punishment. But once she tells me that her brother was also involved I teach her a new lesson. I believe that as the elder she ought to give leadership. Sometimes, her protest comes too early – just at the point when I want to punish her brother. Once she draws attention to her brother, I let the boy off the hook. Don't criticize me, I am learning on the job.

I believe President Obasanjo is in a similar situation with regard to the war against corruption. He has been accused of selective justice; of pretending to be holier than thou; hypocrisy and all you can imagine. Some have even condemned him for starting the war late. You hear such statements like; "why is he just waking up." I would like to think that the important thing is that he has started the fight and he is demonstrating quite some courage. The issues should be whether an individual is guilty or not, not whether he or she is an Atiku person or whether or not Obasanjo is after his enemies only. It is shameful enough to be caught stealing but for the thief and his friends to feel justified simply because there are other better known thieves is rather inexcusable. We are politicking too much with the issue of corruption.

We seem not to know when to stop politics and start governance. Dariye was caught red handed in London and he is today a hero of the same people he defrauded. Alamieyeseigha is also in trouble and some people are threatening to burn down the country. Don't we have any shame anymore? When Tafa Balogun and the Seventeen Billion Naira Saga blew open, some eminent Nigerians started trouping to Abuja to appeal to Obasanjo to forgive him. One is also miffed that some Ijaw leaders are trying to get the President to give Alamieyeseigha a so-called soft landing. Traditional rulers are particularly gifted in begging for the release of thieves. Well, what would you do if you share in the malfeasance? Tafa may yet one day return home triumphant and a hero of sorts. Are we such a shameless people? If we justify our own people when they loot, why must we complain that the country is corrupt? No matter how imperfect and ridiculously selective the current fight is, we must support it and find ways of eliminating the imperfections instead of looking out for opportunities to ridicule the present effort.

The truth is, if the President is selective, it will be at his own peril, because sooner than later, some other people will start the process of selecting him and his men. The immunity clause is the biggest obstacle in the fight against corruption. Governors are the chief thieves in the land today. It is quite instructive that there has been no single demonstration against any governor. Can you imagine the message we would be sending if Nigerians were to demonstrate in support of the detention of Alamieyeseigha?

We need to understand that governors are the greatest creators of poverty and under-development in Nigeria today. They virtually can steal without any control. They amass enormous wealth with which they control not only their various houses of assembly but also their political parties. We must check their excesses. The national assembly is ineffective because a good number of those there are either boys of governors or they are simply their puppets or afraid of them. Three instruments will be important in neutralizing the overbearing influence of governors. The first is the elimination of immunity against criminal conduct; the second is the adoption of a single term for the President and Governors.

If a governor sponsors an entire assembly and keeps them in line with bribes, he soon leaves office and those who are left in the assembly will not feel beholden to the new governor. In a matter of years, we will end up with super legislators who cannot be intimidated by any governor. The third thing we need to do is to free Local Government Areas from the grips of governors. But in the meantime, since we have not been able to do these things, the present course of action by the EFCC should be intensified. It is quite easy to track funds and investments. Money laundering is a broad offence, which demands that the suspect provides proof of the sources of funds, income and investment. EFCC should focus internally on real estate. Local Government officials especially are all over the country building houses like weaver birds. So also are public office holders. An individual, whose total income in thirty years of service is a little over fifteen million naira ought to justify the source of income for the purchase of a twelve million naira house. We don't need to find any evidence of stealing. We need to invoke money-laundering laws to compel people to show how they acquired their incomes. Even if such individuals are so smart, taxation laws should be used as a third layer instrument in the fight against corruption. I don't think we are as yet invoking our tax laws.

25 September, 2005

CHAPTER TWENTY-FIVE

ALAMIEYESEIGHA GOES TO LONDON

The name Alamieyeseigha is a corruption of the English expression: "(Its) all a mess here". If you say this expression with a fast tempo, it sounds quite like the Ijaw name! The Commander General has been captured in London for petty crimes and is having an extended holiday. He was said to have gone to Germany for surgery and got into trouble on his way back. I hope that he did not go to Germany to be operated of *Nairosis*. Obviously, the operation was unsuccessful. I hope Nigerians are not getting scared by the orchestrated threats of violence. Only those who benefit from corruption complain when a thief is captured. I hope he is kept long enough in London for winter. Every day for Mr Thief.

25 September, 2005

CHAPTER TWENTY-SIX

THE RETURN OF ALAMIEYESEIGHA

Nigeria is once again in the news for notoriety. A Governor of one of the states in Nigeria jumped bail in U.K. and you imagine how low people can fall? I have tried to understand what was going on in Alamieyeseigha's mind that caused him to consider the very cheap option and costly way out of his predicament. It is really difficult to imagine a reasonable cause, even though an eminent learned citizen has tried to justify Alamieyeseigha's course of action.

What is clear from the present action is that the man is not a fit and proper person to hold the exalted office of Governor and Nigerians should so declare him unfit through appropriate legal means. It would have been more honourable for him to go to jail because many people would have considered him a victim of persecution. To jump bail is a sign of dishonour. We already have one fugitive as Governor in Nigeria, to have another one is to run the credibility of this nation aground.

When I heard that the man had returned, I was not deceived by stories told about his disguise. I was more appalled by the British Security and Government that have once again chosen to play politics with the image of the black person. It is annoying to say the least that the British Government did not have the courage to let the man go honourably but have to contrive an escape.

This is purely a matter of suspicion on my part, for I cannot understand how this can happen, when they fought so hard to deny him bail and given the measures put in place to check his movement, it is unthinkable that he could so easily beat the British Security. What has happened in my opinion is that Britain took a simple pragmatic business decision to protect their citizens and investments in the Niger Delta and allow Nigeria deal with its own problems.

Unfortunately, this has been done at great cost to our image and credibility. What is even more annoying is that they chose not to warn the Nigerian Government. If really Alamieyeseigha escaped as it is claimed, then Britain is a very unsafe place to live in.

Now that Alamieyeseigha is back, it is now for the people of Bayelsa to impeach him. This time, it should not be for money laundering since there is yet no conviction, but for jumping bail. To have him continue as a Governor will amount to criminal indulgence on the part of Bayelsians. Fools die many times before their death.

27 November, 2005

CHAPTER TWENTY-SEVEN

THE CARTOON MAYHEM

The last few weeks have been very disturbing all over the world. Apart from the spate of bombings in Iraq which we have all become so familiar with, Nigeria had three dishonourable mentions in the press. For a brief moment, even in the local press, the third term agenda was forced out of the top ten charts. If the third term issue had been a musical, by now Obasanjo would be a billionaire. Last month MEND was rather capricious. Soon after the earlier hostage incident there was another more engaging one. With each incident, the hostage takers are getting better and the rhetoric is becoming disturbingly professional. In fact the methods of engagement are becoming really terrifying. They now understand the value of publicity and they know how to get the attention of the world. I am afraid indeed that soon the affair will graduate from a simple business or political transaction to plain sadistic terror. If we get there, then, negotiations will be meaningless because terror will become an end in itself not a means to an end.

The Niger Delta problem must be engaged historically, culturally and politically. Force will surely fail, and when it fails it will be too late to remedy. Today's piece is not going to be about the delta. I will like to reflect on the killer cartoon. Before then let me mention quickly that bird flu was one of the big news item that will be around for a while. Many people have stopped eating chicken and eggs. I will like to request those who have chickens and eggs to part with, that I am one of those who would appreciate a kind gesture. Your free birds and eggs will be gladly received and eaten with appreciation. Let us now talk about the orgy of violence, arson and murder arising from the cartoon of the Prophet. I was amazed to see the violence on TV all over the world. How can a piece of cartoon create such furore? As usual, it took a different colour in Northern Nigeria. It led to the killing of Christians and burning of churches. In faraway Denmark, an agnostic or free thinking irreligious individual cartoons the prophet and in Nigeria, Christians are killed and their churches are burnt. What is the connection? Some individual steps on a page from the Quran or has a quarrel with a Muslim and makes some remarks about the holy book, he or she is beheaded and it is followed by an orgy of killing and arson because the holy book has been desecrated. It often turns out that Ibos are at the receiving end. Reprisal attacks against innocent peaceful Northern Muslims, has become a norm in the East. Islam is increasingly getting a bad name all over the world as a result of the activities of extremists. One is amazed at the ease with which Muslims get provoked to violence. One issue that is being debated today as a result of the current situation is the limits of freedom of expression.

Where does personal liberty stop? There is now an increasing intersection between personal space and Islamic space. Some decades ago, Salma Rushdie was condemned to death for his work and it took diplomacy and arm twisting to lift the Fatwa. We have had the Akaluka case and the Lady journalist who was hounded out for an innocent mistake at worst. I have tried to find out how many in Nigeria actually saw the cartoon. Certainly, it is doubtful if many among those who went out to kill in Nigeria know what a cartoon is let alone seen the offensive cartoon. Having said this however, it is important to state that given the current political climate in the world journalists and creative writers must display the highest sense of responsibility and respect for those who are different no matter how much in error we think they are. Western intellectuals and writers need to be sensitive to the beliefs of other people. They need to be educated about different cultures and their values. We all see life from different angles and no one has a right to denigrate other cultures.

There is a certain level of arrogance that drives people to disregard the feelings of other people in the name of freedom of speech and constitutional rights. In the modern global environment it should be clear that no one can take the excuse of his or her national laws to assault the world of other people. There are consequences when this is done and we are living witnesses of this. Christians have suffered more than Muslims from attempts by western film makers, writers and artists to denigrate Christ and Christianity. But they do not go about burning houses or killing people. One is sometimes inclined to believe that the disregard for culture and beliefs of other people is driven more by a commercial spirit than by creativity. Freedom of speech cannot be a license to injure the feelings of others. Issues of culture and religion must be handled responsibly. The press must show the highest level of sensitivity as regards what is put in public domain. We are all very familiar with how African cultures are denigrated in the literature when common practices are labelled with demeaning terms. For instance, Africans talk about female circumcision, western science talks about genital mutilation. The Yoruba talk about beauty marks, the literature talks about scarification. Whether we talk about rituals or worship, sacrifice or offering in religious setting, our choice of words betray a value judgment and a bias. Let us return to the cartoon. If the cartoon was intended to provoke Muslims, it certainly succeeded.

This is where I really feel sorry for the millions of peace loving Muslims who are now being labelled as violent. It doesn't make sense that one man, one newspaper insults Muslims and the whole world is called to pay. Has anyone determined the complicity of the Danish government let alone all the Europeans, Americans and Nigerian Christians? Watching the riots it is clear that western interests are the target. It is only in Nigeria that we have twisted it again and have attacked our own people. Some of our politicians have tried to blame the third term agenda for the riots. How pedestrian can we get? How does a third term by Obasanjo become a Christian agenda? What happened in the last few weeks is disgraceful and should be condemned. Those who organized the violence should be punished and restitutions made where possible.

5 March, 2006

CHAPTER TWENTY-EIGHT

ASHEWO POLITICS

There was an interesting discussion in my staff club the other day. Some people were lamenting over the revelations made by Atiku relating to the use of Government money to service expensive *Ashewo* in London. One young man related the plight of a top banker who was compelled to deliver 200,000usd weekly to a lady. The interesting part was that there were two ladies with us at the table. We thought they were students or relatives of someone in the club. Of course you know that club environments are usually a nest of vices. The two girls were actually *along the road girls* or *bushmeat* in another parlance. How did we find out? One young man kept on railing out against Ashewo in politics. One of the girls became so offended at the term that she almost pounced on the young man. At one point the argument became so base that I just hoped that my Pastor will not walk in. Let us avoid the lurid details and focus on the conclusion.

I was able to gather that the word Ashewo is cheap and that some people are better referred to as *Ashedollars* or *Ashepound*. The local term is reserved for the naira hunters and the miserable roadside prostitute. If we are really serious about cleaning up our politics we ought to examine the Ashewo Factor in the polity. We need to get down to the family life of political office holders, their perception of women and moral standing. It is public knowledge that women are served as Suya at political forums. Young girls in higher institutions are herded every weekend and allocated as ice cream to our politicians. For your information, that is currently the most profitable business around. Infidelity is a requirement for political success in Nigeria.

I am often amused to see women fight for increased representation and power while failing to check the sexual abuse of teenagers by political office holders and sick old men in high places. I think leadership must begin here. Who of us know how many wives or mistresses our President, his vice, the Governors, etc. have? We are told that embassies now have a hard time designating the numerous ladies with diplomatic passports from Nigeria. There is now a term for them: *PFP*, *PFVP*, *PFG*, these mean, **pregnant for the president; pregnant for the vice president, pregnant for a Governor**. Wouldn't it be nice to know how many wives and children our president and his vice have? Is there any record anywhere? If one's family life is not a good measure of integrity, I wonder what is. Public office holders should now be required to declare their wives, along with their assets and their "Ex-s" along with their liabilities. New acquisitions in office should also be made public. I don't think it will be out of place to forbid them from having **foreign female accounts (FFA)** for security reasons. It is so easy to deal with men if you hold them by their balls.

The other side of corruption is the issue of false declaration of assets. A one-time Governor in the South West was said to have declared his assets upfront and he proceeded to acquire them once he got to office. Declared assets of public office holders should be available to the public. They should also be required to provide evidence of the source of their wealth. It is only in this country that rich people emerge overnight. A man can go out a pauper and return home a whiz kid or a mogul. People get rich without any employment. This tendency has created the consciousness in our youths that wealth comes suddenly by deals and miracles. If we ask people to justify their wealth before applying for public office, ninety eight percent of those currently seeking public office will decline. The stupendous wealth of the current crop of army generals and civil servants are simply loots. No matter how many followers they have, or names given to them, they are petty thieves. If anyone does not want the public to pry into his or her private life he should not seek public office. We have a divine right as employers of public office holders to scrutinize their CV and determine if they are fit and proper individuals. It is not enough for these people to just declare assets for the records and for *EFCC* and *ICPC* to wait for petitions. People must justify their wealth. We must now insist on minimums for integrity. We need truly religious individuals; those who are religious from head to toe, not those whose religion does not apply from their waist down. We don't need those who stir up religious sentiments in order to prevent scrutiny.

The *Obj/Atiku* match is very revealing indeed. It is clear that Atiku ate with both hands and therefore cannot shake hands with the law. Obasanjo on the other hand forgot to clean his mouth and so he has a problem with foul breath. Both of them are singing Fela's song: "you be thief, I no be thief, you be robber, I no be robber". It appears as if Atiku is saying that he is not the only thief around and Obj is saying that he only borrowed some money without following due process.

The Ekiti saga is an eye opener to all. No condition is permanent. The Governor's name has changed again as we have been told. He started as Fayose; "Ifa will do it" and became Oluwayose; "God will do it". Now his name is Fayo8se?; "Ifa has withdrawn his support" literally, *Ifa has removed his leg.*

8 October, 2006

CHAPTER TWENTY-NINE

POWER SHIFT: OPTIONS FOR 2007

I thought I had said the last word on the issue of power shift; but developments over the last one or two weeks has forced me into putting in what I hope will be the last comment before the unravelling of the knot. The Sunday tribune of 8th January 2006 had as one of its headlines: North counters South again; Holds meeting Thursday. Then of course Saraki was said to have stated that the North will fight the South to a standstill. A few things need to be stated clearly. Politicians like Saraki often speak for a people they really do not care about. I really will like to know which North he speaks for – the oligarchy or the common people. The current sectional divide arising from the issue of power shift shows clearly how terribly misleading our so-called political heavyweights can be. I have spoken with a cross section of Nigerians from different regions and social backgrounds, it would seem that across ethnic groups and regions there is a fair agreement that President Obasanjo should leave in 2007.The problem however is that the 3rd term agenda is being confused with the issue of power shift. Consequently there is a gradual erosion of the unity against a third term agenda. It will be interesting to see which South the Northern politicians are going to be battling to a standstill. It is too late now not to have a crisis in 2007. It is also too late for President Obasanjo to leave honorably. Even if he announces today that he is leaving tomorrow, Nigerians will boo him. There is a time for everything under the sun. One's biggest headache now is whether the census will hold or should hold. If it does, it is most unlikely that authentic figures will be declared.

These days are some of my saddest. The impeachment of Governor Ladoja has just been wangled through and Oyo Government house is in the hands of questionable characters. I am sad because I pay my taxes here. I am even sadder because taxes here are very high. I can't believe that I will be delivering over 15% of my salary monthly to *Molete*. Who on earth is the new Governor? What do we know about his past? Oyo state is going into the abyss and the people are in the market place thinking that they are immune. Let us return to the issue. But before then, I will like to say that a useful lesson should be learnt by those who must attain power at all cost. There is another reason why I am sad for this country. We are again reducing serious issues of development to such trivialities as power shift. For me, it is trivial because ordinarily, these are matters that free and fair elections should settle. Another reason why I consider it trivial is the fact that we still cannot articulate an effective response to the AIDS pandemic. We are still burying our women from maternal death, we are losing our children in their millions to malaria and diarrhoea. It is annoying to see the same breed of shameless inheritors of our country gather once more to sound the drums of war over who should control the Naira. Power shift is nothing more than the struggle over the control of oil. Those who are weeping the loudest have had three decades to transform this country but they have only transformed themselves, their children and their harems. I ran through the list of those who congregated in the Southern leaders meeting. They are those who got money to pave roads to their states but paved their foreign accounts. Among them are those who got rich from serving Abacha. Look at the gathering in the North. They are either recycled or unrecyclable politicians, failed politicians, failed bank crooks or bitter individuals.

I mentioned elsewhere that the case of the North for power shift is weak on grounds of morality and equity. But even then, it is only at the elections that power should shift. To heat up the polity over this issue is an indication of the moral corruption of a cross section of our politicians. We all seem to have accepted that as always, there will be no elections but a selection in 2007. This is a tragedy and a pointer to what the future holds for the country. In a sane clime politicians should be properly focused on how to ensure free and fair elections. Our politicians don't believe in elections. How else could one explain the enormous power that witch doctors and political thugs wield in our polity? This is why confirmed daft become princes in our political process. I was amused to hear that the reins of power in one of the South west states was virtually surrendered to a seer. People don't believe they need to rule well to retain power, neither do they believe that good politics wins elections. So, they either join cults, sleep under Iroko trees, kill for human sacrifice or do something as silly as sleeping with their daughter to win elections. Disgusting vermin!

Today the politics is all about the so-called 3rd term agenda of Mr President. The man also appears to be enjoying the limelight. What I find most interesting is that every action of the President is now interpreted in the contest of a 3rd term agenda. If a known thief is caught people scream that it is because he is against the agenda. I feel sorry for the man because if he truly preoccupies himself with such matters as some claim, he certainly will end up like the proverbial elephant who fell into a hole disguised to trap him. Selective justice is now a phrase most Nigerians are familiar with. Some time ago, Marwa was OBJ's friend we are told. Today he is a victim. Fasawe was a friend of the President, now he is an enemy par excellence. Who knows it may be Bode George or Anenih next. I like the kind of vendetta that leads a person to jail a friend for breaking the law. I want to hear that those who have been jailed so far are innocent and are being victimized. To scream injustice when a thief is condemned because there are more eminent thieves is corrupt. I think one reason people feel unmoved by the current fight against corruption is the way the Osuji saga ended without the head of the ES of NUC. The man seems to be getting bigger by the day. Let us not be naïve. Everyone has his soft spots and there are those reserved for burial with a king. Time catches up with everyone. In this country no evil one will sleep until we are all squeaky clean. Power will change hands and rewards and punishments will be apportioned accordingly.

So what are the possible options for 2007? If we are serious about development and peace, we should run a true federation and decentralize. But not so. True federation will not materialize because those who are in a position to ensure equity and justice are dominated by self-interest and overcome by short-sighted frothing for power. Will OBJ hand over in 2007? Anyone's guess. I am not a prophet. Should he? Capital yes! Suppose by fire by force he has to handover? Let us work with the polity we know not the one we expect. There will be much flood in 2006 and fire will fall from the sky. The sun of politics will be eclipsed, but the house will stand. If the house stands, then the sun will rise again. Whose sun? Time will tell. Let us look to possibilities that the oligarchy will be broken. Let us look to the probability that a young shoot will grow out of the new plant. Let us imagine that good governance will arise. Don't we have a right to dream? PDP will rig. But this notwithstanding, they will calm the storm, then a child king may be raised high by the lion king on Zuma rock. If we look at the stars they say one thing. If we cast the oracle they speak a different language. If you listen to your heart you hear many things. What then do we do? Have faith and pray.

15 January, 2006

CHAPTER THIRTY

THE DILEMMA OF A GHOST

I sat watching the *NTA* on one of those rare days recently and I heard a disclaimer from the Rivers State Governor over a news item in a newspaper. The governor was purported to have said that "term extension was a crazy idea." I actually agree with him and so do many Nigerians. But Odili, the Governor denied the report as the work of detractors and those who are trying to breach the good relationship between the Rivers Government and the Federal Government. These were not his exact words. First, I was puzzled because I couldn't fathom how a harmless platitude like that could constitute a problem to the Federal Government. After all we have been told that Mr President has not expressly declared interest in a third term, life term or whatever one may call it. Perhaps the problem was really not that Odili did not make such a statement but that the word, extension was used. If you have been following developments closely, you would realize that even though the president does not want to breach the constitution, he is not averse to term extension.

By the elaborate denial by someone as close to power as Odili, it is no longer a matter or speculation that someone is still interested in throne of Abuja. Isn't it a shame that the only business going on in the country today is the so called third term? There are already some fruits from the project. The handover of Charles Taylor and the Stakeholders forum for the Niger Delta are two benefits from the agenda. Who doesn't need friends? Let us not move too far away from the mark. I was engaged recently by someone who is obviously a third term lover. Please, forgive me; I think we have actually crossed the 3rd line we should actually be talking about life line. The man asked me to name one Nigerian who can fit into Obasanjo's shoes. Well obviously, as I said, there is no one. But I told him that I know of an individual who could be President of Nigeria. He braced up with all the usual arguments. He was in for the shock of his life. He expected me to begin to mention such names of expired and irredeemable leaders like Babangida, Buhari, Marwa and what have you. If not he was expecting me to mention the young and celebrated members of the present cabinet. Well, I told him that if there was no one available, I am eminently qualified to be president of Nigeria. What you think about this is your palaver. Constitutionally speaking and by my credentials I, or any other Nigerian for that matter who feels able to serve, is qualified to replace Obasanjo as the president of the country. Of course he laughed me to scorn. Here lies the problem. The fact that Nigerians do not really want the kind of change they call for. What were my failings in his estimation? I do not have the money or the clout to get people to follow. Here again I disagreed. If it is a question of clean money, I am sure that I will raise more money than any of the current gladiators. If it is a matter of clout, there is no doubt in my mind that I will cause even the trees to follow. I told him that my limitation is that I cannot descend to the low limits of rigging an election or plundering national resources to gain power. Power in Nigeria is attained by fraud and sustained by brute force.

There is no politics in this country because there are no rules and no competition. I was reminded that Nigeria is complex and that as a civilian I cannot control the Army. These reasons I consider really childish since I cannot see the complexity in the country, except that which has been created by inequities and exaggerated by official corruption. The army is made up of people who have relatives and come from places. They go to the same markets as we all do and feel what we feel. The greatest safeguard to security is not by bribing top military officials but by ensuring economic prosperity and social justice. I think it is particularly important for Nigerians to start declaring their interest in the top job and stop acting scared like children who are afraid of the dark.

The so called big politicians are all falling over themselves to line up behind Obasanjo as if he is God.

They are scared to come out to declare their interest because of their past ways of error. They all want the approval of the incumbent as that will mean that their sins will be covered up and they will be guaranteed the use of the army and police in rigging. None of them qualifies to be President of Nigeria. They are lily-livered gold diggers. Now what are the options before Nigerians considering that many do not want to break away from the corrupt past? People have touted Marwa as a possible alternative. But why has he gone dead quiet? A man who would rule should not be afraid of dying for his convictions. Truth is he does not believe in anything but money. He is also scared stiff of EFCC. What about Buhari. He cannot make a good leader considering his vulnerability regarding religious issues. He will be a divisive, sectional and religious leader. IBB? If this man happens on Nigeria, I will surely know that we are a people who do not deserve peace. The man will surely get the politicians together by the instrument of monetary persuasion. What new tricks can an old horse learn? We do not need people from the past.

It is time to get a new breed, a thorough bred. I don't know who will emerge to start our new republic. Whoever that person will be, he or she must be courageous, squeaky clean, intellectually able, balanced and ready to sacrifice all for this country. Now should Atiku be? Apart from the fact that he is too rich and needs to tell us how he came into his money, he will give us more of the same. He also will need a second and third term. He will have to set up his own EFCC to try Obj's men; if not he will forgive all their sins ostensibly as a sign of magnanimity when in reality he will just be trying to ensure that he starts off without competition. A third term for Obasanjo will translate into a life term. Is he known to keep his promise? The Bible talks of a person keeping his promise even to his own hurt. One reason why we are told that it may be necessary to break rules and promises is that God does not like abandoned projects. Whose projects and who has abandoned it?

There is no doubt that there are benefits in continuity. But is it not true also that the test of a successful leadership is that followers willingly continue in the footsteps of their leader? Is it not also a vote of no confidence or even a failure of character for a person to be in a position for years and cannot find even one individual he can trust? It is a shame indeed that even those who should inherit the position are wallowing in the mud of disclaimer issued against them by their leader. I will tell you the story of the Lion who ruled the forest and had no successor because none of the lionesses had a male cub. All animals lived knowing that the jungle must be ruled by a lion. None ever thought he could inherit the throne. When it was getting close to the time of the ancestors, the baboon, who advises the Lion, told him to introduce *Nkite*, a very strong Lioness as his successor. But he will not because of traditions whose origin no one remembered. He kept on trying for male children until the age of the wilderness set in. The king was now faced with a dilemma, how to die peacefully and who to hand power over to. At the first sign of weakness in a king lion, other wild creatures attacked and devoured him and scattered his pride. He decided to call each wild creature that could be a threat in secret and promise him the throne.

The rule was that such a creature will forfeit the throne if any person got to know of it before the appointed time. So, everyone went about in delusion doing in the other and out doing one another. When all wild ones gathered around him, he realized that he needed not go far any more to hunt. He started to feed on them. He reasoned that he could satisfy his hunger and reduce the threats by eating the wild ones. Very soon the forest was low in hunters and common creatures multiplied exceedingly. He got his statue made so that people will start relating to it and he will come out sparingly. It was a good trick to ensure his immortality. When he dies eventually, people will not know because they will be used to relating to the statue. That was not to be because the birds could see what was going on from the sky. How would we get rid of him seeing that we have no weapons they reasoned? Well said the vulture let us get all the animals to attack him while he is asleep. The owl said with one fierce roar everyone will disperse and poor creatures will be punished.

Moreover, how can we gather so many together without it leaking knowing that some even among us work for him? It was the dove who knew what to do but he will not speak. He could only trust the thunder. He pleaded with him to roar on an uncommon day when animals are foraging and the lion is nearby with his wild ones ready to hunt. The roar will cause a stampede in the direction of the lion and his party. That way, without meaning to, he and his clan will be wiped away. It was a great thunder that bright evening and the stampede was unprecedented because the animals thought the sky was falling down. The mass of the wildebeest, the deer, Rhino and all creatures trampled the lion underfoot with the wild ones. Afterwards when there was calm and the news went round that the lion was gone with his clan and wild ones, the jungle rejoiced. The dove was asked to lead because he was the most peaceful and less likely of all creatures to destroy the forest. They all agreed to submit to his leadership. But they never knew that he was responsible for the stampede. A boring story, but I hope there is a lesson there. Obasanjo's dilemma at this point is like that of a ghost. A ghost is a ghost and is a ghost no matter what we try to make of it. The reality of a ghost itself is a matter for speculation. The more so because it cannot make its own case or would not and even if it tried, the fact that it is confined to the dark and the nether world does not help its case. He is neither with the living nor with the dead.

26 April, 2006

Francis Egbokhare

CHAPTER THIRTY-ONE

THE MONKEY GOES TO SCHOOL

The events in the Nigerian political scene in the last few weeks, has filled me with so much worry and excitement to the extent that I felt that I should enlist in a monastery as a monk. One is really ashamed that we are going round in circles of repeated failure. Could anyone have imagined that Mr Mclean will be associated in any way with bribery for whatever reason? Whatever good Obasanjo has done in the last seven years have been wasted in the alter of ambition. It is a shame that he will end up like the rest before him who were disgraced out of power. I was really amazed at the animal boldness of the PDP Chairman and his secretary who assumed that they were Garrison commanders. The defeat of the third term agenda reminds me of a village tyrant I know somewhere. This man was so powerful and feared that many people had come to believe that he had some mystical powers. He went about beating and intimidating fellow villagers. He was followed because people feared him. Then one day, one very day as it goes in all tragic tales, he met this weakling whose only offense was that everyone in the village knew that his wife flogged him regularly.

Well, there was a misunderstanding. Everyone tried to pacify the strong man but he will not be assuaged. As he swung a terrible right punch meant to deflate the weakling, he slipped and landed hard on the floor. He could not rise so the weakling sat on him and fed him a good meal of wet sand. The story went round the village that he had been beaten by the most unexpected individual. Within a few days many more people had challenged him in the most ridiculous of circumstances and of course, each time he got a good thrashing. He became the threshing floor of the village. When a strong man falls, he does not fall lightly. When a tyrant is disgraced, it is to proverbial magnitude. One thing that shocked me during the last few weeks was the reinjection of the virus called Nzeribe into our politics. Those who claim that the president means well cannot be serious. How can you be bribing and manipulating and arresting the opposition and clamping down on the press so viciously and mean well? The Abacha type advertisements reappeared in the television to ones dismay. What happened to the third term agenda will lead to many more beatings for the president. Not only he, but also his henchmen will now have to experience the cold shame of seeing political nonentities defy them openly. Soon they will be like the village prostitute that every young man must sleep with to prove that he is of age. The president has been demystified. When a masquerade is unmasked, it is often better for the mask man to flee the village because there will be reprisals from those he whipped under the protection of the ancestors. I believe that we all can learn that money and threats will not always win. Politics of control has failed and people power is being enthroned. PDP is ruined whether they realize it or not. This is the end of the road for those who believed that they had the country in their pockets because they had become close to the corridors of power. Many will gnash their teeth in the last days and political lives of several people will come to a premature end. We expect more dramatic things to happen if the Atiku camp wishes to seize the initiative. We expect a reintroduction of the impeachment procedures. On the other side it will be expected for the president's men to seek to abort the political ambition of those perceived to be behind the saga. More corruption revelation may turn up.

Now the struggle will really begin between the three gladiators in the scene. There will be no governance between now and the elections. Those who have not amassed enough may well decide to fill their coffers because of the uncertainty ahead. I must at this point agree with those who say that the real casualty are the over 100 proposals for amendment of the constitution. There is no doubt that we needed to amend the constitution. But a responsible and patriotic president would not have tried to exploit the people's genuine desire for a review to push his own agenda to become a life president. It is the president and his men, not the national assembly who should take the blame. I believe that the president still has an opportunity to redeem his image by organizing a credible election in 2007. Clearly, any attempt by this PDP to rig elections as they did previously will be met with disaster. If the elections are free, Nigerians will forget his many schemes. After all we have very short memories. I will like also to warn the national assembly not to go to sleep after this. They must seize this initiative to correct some anomalies in our electoral and judicial laws. If however some of them think that they have gained the upper hand in the political equation, they will only be living in a fool's paradise. The assembly spent the best part of seven years haggling over money and changing its leadership. If they are smart, this is the time to wean themselves from executive control and manipulation. The most important event we are all expecting is a free and fair elections. People power will only come when the vote of the ordinary man counts. Now a final word for the manipulators and those fixers in our midst. **One day monkey go go market e no go return.** I wish to take this opportunity to inform readers of this column that from the first week in June, I will go on hibernation. It is time to audit and edit my life. I wish to thank you all for being with me and for your comments. The Nigerian Tribune gave me a free hand to express myself. I am grateful for the opportunity to serve my country through the column. My gratitude goes most especially to the Editor and team of Sunday Tribune.

2 January, 2006

CHAPTER THIRTY-TWO

FIDDLERS ON THE ROOF

If you followed the conventions of the three major parties in the last two weeks like I did, you will be glad and sad at the same time. Glad that nemesis reincarnated in Nigeria and sad that democracy was turned upside down. Some of my friends argue that we should be glad and accept the outcome no matter how flawed because Rome was not built in a day. I would agree with them to the extent that progress takes time to actualize. I however am not so sure that we are building any real structures. I wish again to agree with another friend who believes that the current administration has done some good work. Actually, even Abacha did well in some areas. We are told in school that no child is a total failure. You may be strong in some subjects and terribly weak in others. We can point to some gains in the economy: foreign direct investment, consolidation of banks, introduction of GSM, payment of Nigeria's foreign debt. We can also point to the work of NAFDAC, EFCC, SON and of course the huge foreign reserves. We can point to several other areas of failure: bad roads, worse power situation, assassinations and unsolved murders, escalating robberies and general insecurity, failed national identity scheme, problems in the aviation sector and air crashes, escalation of violence in the Niger Delta, mass poverty, widening gap between the poor and rich, political instability, official disrespect for the rule of law among other things.

On a scale of average I think we do not exactly have a pass situation. In assessing this regime, we often forget that we have had the unique opportunity in history to earn so much more than we budgeted for. Yet we have been so lacking in translating our surplus to development and wealth for our people. If we cannot manage surplus, how can we manage scarcity? Each new government in Nigeria appears to push the limits of politics. I believe that with the demise of Abacha, Nigerians thought we had seen the last of impunity. Alas we all now realize that hell is a bottomless pit. The only thing that has not happened in Nigeria is a military incursion or war situation. I think we all need to congratulate ourselves for avoiding the train of war. I do not watch Television a lot. I can hardly stand what is put up as news, whether by CNN, NTA or the local stations. What particularly irks me is the amount of time spent on singing the praises of deluded politicians and opening projects which we all know are overvalued, not to talk of the fact that most cease to work moments after they are commissioned. Let us look at the areas where the government has succeeded. These are organizations driven by a few committed individuals. Characteristically, the black man celebrates people too early, so they become useless to themselves and society. Let a backyard footballer score a goal and he is described as a soccer star. All of a sudden, a person can come from the blues and declare himself a billionaire and in our characteristic laziness we will all soon address him as a whiz kid. Then we all start running after his money. We harvest our best brains before they mature and abort good ideas even before they take root. Talking about areas where some successes has been recorded, NAFDAC and EFCC are two examples, but both organizations are driven by personalities not structures or the system.

Their work is likely to end with their current leaders. Is that how progress should be made? The individuals themselves started very humbly, but as always happens in the country of the blind, they are beginning to take on messianic roles. We have praised and decorated them so much that they are beginning to look like moving statues. We kill our good people with false love and dubious appreciation. Most of what is going on in our country today that we are applauding is still too much of memory work. There are too many noise makers and people holding positions that are bigger than them.

The conventions of the parties are a reflection of the failure of our politics. Why are people afraid of elections? We have invented dictatorship by consensus. The events remind me of two Bini chiefs who wanted to find out who among the two-some was the more intelligent. 1+1 asked one of them. 3 replied the other. "I thought you will miss it" said the questioner. Then both of them hugged each other for being so brilliant unlike the other chiefs. The emergence of Yar Adua as the PDP "fag" bearer has thrown up a lot of speculations. If so, the choice of Goodluck has created even more reason for unease. Someone described the combination as eating Tuwo with Salad. Ordinarily, if both of them make it, this will be the first time we will be having University graduates as president and vice. In fact we all ought to have rejoiced that we did not again end up with a military candidate. The shine in the combination was robbed by the process that produced them and doubts about the ticket. Both of them are drafts. There is palpable fear that once more the era of led-leadership is back. There are reasons to believe that the third term agenda has been realized through the ticket. Obasanjo is likely to become the ventriloquist who will speak through a Yar puppet. Why not? The amendments to the PDP constitution will make this a fait accompli. Will Adua mime Oba's voice? Are we going to end up with a weak president? I really do not want to speculate because I still have my doubts about 2007. I will prefer a weak president to not having a transition at all. But let us look at the true winners at the conventions; Katsina state and PDM. Whether in Atiku or Yar Adua, PDM remains the true owner of Nigerian politics. Obj loses. Whether in Buhari or Adua, Katsina is the winner. I think that once the advantage so shifts, after the elections, the permutations will change and other factors will determine how the ticket behaves, if it wins. PDP will no longer be the basis or platform that will guide the flow of power. Amendments of constitution will be useless with the enormity of the powers available to the office of the Nigerian President. I am sure that the PDP flag bearer is learning from the display of naked power by the President. He can also see that with the military and police behind one, there is no need for the constitution. Jonathan or any VP must now understand that he is a dog and must only lick the Boss' behind. If Yar Adua was ever with Bala, I am sure that he will be a good student of history and power. Being taciturn will then be used to effect as a disguise to confuse those who seek always to enthrone weaklings. Absolute power corrupts absolutely, not just that, those who enthrone a king are the first victims of his naked power.

I believe that we all can learn from the fall of Babangida. If Yar Adua is a true brother of the general, he obviously has learnt how to act the power script. In all, I think the true loser is President Obasanjo. The fiddler has fiddled with his own peace. The monkey has gone to the market and may not return home. As is the pattern of modern dictators he is likely to go for reorientation somewhere far away. As is the pattern of former leaders accused of corruption, we may have an opportunity to see the hunter hunted. Let us take a cue from Zambia. If the elections are free and fair, we could have another party in power. But Nigerians should not expect much change in the polity. The conventions have shown that the struggle is not about democracy or rule of law, but about advantage and power to corner resources. I cannot see AC or ANPP doing much better than the PDP. The good thing however is that the days of landslide victory is gone. Remember Rivers State? Are you sad that Odili lost? I am so glad that a lesson has been learnt. Woe unto those who trust in men! This was a man who virtually served himself and "the party". Port Harcourt is a sorry sight, in spite of the huge resources the state got over the last eight years, poverty rules. Those who supported the third term agenda have seen that it is more profitable to stay with the people than to follow blind ambition. The south-south leaders must be suffering from political stroke. They need a political doctor to keep their hearts beating. For many, this is the end of politics. I wonder if Jerry Gana still believes that Obasanjo is the father of modern Nigeria. Must we call a cow a brother so we can eat beef?

14 January, 2007

CHAPTER THIRTY-THREE

THE LEADER NIGERIA NEEDS

Through wisdom a house is built; and by understanding it is established; by knowledge the rooms are filled with all precious and pleasant riches (Prov. 24: 3, 4). A nation is built by wise people. Men and women of understanding design the processes and structures on which it is established. It takes only knowledgeable individuals to create wealth and prosperity. A wise man understands the difference between riches and prosperity. A nation may be rich and yet not prosperous. A rich nation is one whose balance sheet shows a surplus. A prosperous one is that where citizens live in humane conditions, where the general conditions of life give opportunities for hope and joy. We must move to the next level by deploying our knowledge resources creatively in order to fill our land with riches and prosperity. If we must break the yoke of poverty and overcome the burden of disease; if we would upturn our reproach we need a leader who knows; who understands and has the wisdom to lead with humility and compassion. A wise leader leads by example. He shares in the people's suffering, their shame and joy. He gives hope through his life, he inspires through his character, he instructs through his sacrifice. If the people will carry a burden, he is the first to lift two; if they must starve his children will be first on the list. We have rulers in Nigeria not leaders. They preach reform and pile up farms to feed foreign lands. They fight corruption but fail to check their own greed.

We have dwelt long enough on our mountain of despair. We have stayed too long in the valley of failure. We have swam too long in the floods of crisis and underdevelopment. It is high time we started taking responsibility. We should put our hands together on the plow of national development. Nigeria is the only country we have. Its failure is our failure, its pains are our pains, its gains our gains. Let us focus on the common good; let us deemphasize our differences and look to what unites us. Let us join hands together and make Nigeria the pride of the black race. We are able to do it because we have hope. We can achieve it because we believe we can. We have what it takes. It is time to dream again!

We call on you to share in this new dream, to be part of a great movement; to join the critical mass that will create the greatest change in the history of mankind. Make Nigeria the new EDEN! We can turn our lamentation into joy; we can transform our fears into energy; we can turn our reproach into praise; our grumblings can become prayers; our differences can become our assets; our failings opportunities. Let us build a land where the old can dream and the young see visions. A place, where rich or poor; old or young; weak or strong have a place to stand.

There is a leader for every time. A momentous time needs an extraordinary individual. There is a champion for every vision. A champion stays the course no matter what. A leader understands the times. He understands what must be done and knows how to get things done. A leader is a knowledgeable man, skilled in learning and wisdom.

One may buy fame. Your reputation is who people think you are. But character is a priceless virtue that cannot be faked. It shows and speaks through time and times. Nigeria needs a man of character to lead her, such a person should be:

- ✓ Wise without being crafty
- ✓ Skilful but not manipulative
- ✓ Listens but is not fickle
- ✓ Compassionate but not patronizing
- ✓ Respectful but not servile
- ✓ Strong yet meek
- ✓ Learned but full of humility

- ✓ Firm without being rigid
- ✓ Passionate but not overzealous
- ✓ Enthusiastic but not overbearing
- ✓ Confident but not arrogant
- ✓ Courageous but not foolhardy
- ✓ Focused yet not self-willed.
- ✓ Religious but not fanatical

Ten Qualities Which Our President Must Have

1. **Continuity:** "In which ever way we look at it, Nigeria has come a long way since 1999". It is clear that the principles of reforms and anti-corruption have been pursued even though with tainted zeal by president Obasanjo. The next president should continue to reform. But he must first reform himself. He should move beyond reforms into genuine transformation of our society. Anti-corruption must start with a probe of the current federal government and all the state governments. Nigerians will like to know why fuel scarcity persists in spite of huge expenditure in the repair of refineries. We want to know why the roads remain terrible, why the power sector is unyielding after so much investment. Nigerians want to know how their leaders suddenly became billionaires overnight. Nigerians want to know how their president got the funds with which he bought his farms. Apart from this we want to know who the owners of the numerous transport companies are.

2. **Loyalty:** Loyalty must begin with respect for the constitution and the laws of the land. It is established in one's subjection of his ambition to national interest. The new president must not be a manipulator, a law breaker, a liar, a womanizer, a cultist and an unjust fellow. He must truly fear God in deeds not words alone.

3. **Courage:** True courage is the ability to subject yourself to authority, the ability to restrain yourself from crushing the weak; the understanding of your limitations and a correct evaluation of

your options at any given point. It involves putting yourself at risk for those who have no voice. It is not a function of brute force, an exercise of self-will: But putting yourself at risk for the common good. A truly courageous man puts his life down for his fellow man.

4. **Inspiring Leadership:** A leader is not one who gets people to do what they ordinarily ought to do by threats. He is one for whom people would gladly do those things which they would otherwise not contemplate. The president must be a mobilizer. He should inspire hope. In times like this, when our people are required to make difficult adjustments, they need inspiring leadership.

5. **A Family Man:** Every nation is built on the quality of the family. The family life of a leader is the subject of public debate. A leader with a sound family life is an asset not only to the party but also to the nation in building its core values and focusing on reorienting the national psyche. Nigeria must look to someone with a solid family set up. We cannot again have people lead us who send the wrong signals to our youth.

6. **Qualifications:** The challenges of development in the global arena have become so complex that the leader must be capable of understanding the intricacies of governance and international politics and cooperation. It is now too risky to have individuals learn on the job. The leader must be intellectually sophisticated and skilled to earn respect and command authority. The political space is now global to the point that local political influence is no longer enough.

7. **Nationalist:** What kind of leader do we desire? An ethnic leader promoted to national limelight on the altar of expediency? A religious chauvinist or some individual with questionable means who rides on agitations? We think we need a nationalist with outstanding credentials and legendary experience. We are in a period in history when we cannot afford to make mistakes. This cannot be an era of politics of settlement. We stand the risk of

losing all the gains of democracy if we promote self above the common good; if we insist on entrenched ethnic positions and promote individuals who lack the pedigree.

8. **Experience:** If experience can be measured in depths and span, Nigeria more than ever before needs a leader who is deep and expansive. We need a person who can act as a thread that links the various phases of Nigeria's recent history. A man who has political savvy and is a skilled manager of human and material resources. We do not need an experienced thief, a local chieftain or a discredited brute.

9. **An Excellent Bridge Builder:** We need a bridge; an uncontroversial individual who has links across the length and breadth of the nations. Our President must be a bridge across the nations and generations. A consensus builder, an avid communicator, a listener.

10. **Compassion:** Development is about people. Policies must be given human face and rules and laws must exist for people. The tragic thing about our interpretation of development sometimes is that we are often led to accept foreign paradigms without questioning their relevance and we implement ideas without contextualizing them. Development cannot be trivialized to the point of sloganeering, just as change does not come about because we wish it. At this point in our history, given the severity of poverty and disease, we need a leader who is in touch with the people and their conditions. Poverty will not disappear until the leaders themselves bring their own conditions closer to the people or lift up the people closer to their own conditions.

"The future is not some place we are going to, but one we are creating. The paths are not to found, but made, and the activity of making them changes both the maker and the destination." (John Schaar). If we can dream again, then we can achieve great things. If we could revive hope, then we will arrive at our destinations. We have faith that Nigeria will one day, soon, in our life time become the land of opportunity. A place of unlimited promise for all; an oasis in a world torn apart by crisis; and a pride to all black peoples where ever they are. Who among the current contestants for the office of President knows how to get us to this land of our dreams?

25 February, 2007

CHAPTER THIRTY-FOUR

CHOP CHOP POLITICS

Who can explain to me why an individual will leave a party for another, then cross back to the same party and then leave again for another party? The way politicians are busy moving up and down, it is clear that people are just looking for where to chop. The case of the ANPP Governors is particularly ridiculous. Buhari is now stranded because those who were supposed to support his ambition are now busy in the PDP as candidates. Many have forgotten the caustic criticism they railed against OBJ just a couple of months ago. All of a sudden the party is the best thing that has happened to Nigeria and Obasanjo has become the father of modern Nigeria. With the death of Chief Awolowo, true party politics ended in Nigeria. Ideology ceased with the UPN. What is going on today is simply haggling. We are in a market place trading our national resources in the guise of politics. Take the case of Oyo and Anambra, is anyone in doubt that only confusion and strife will reign in those places in the next four years?

Francis Egbokhare

CHAPTER THIRTY-FIVE

ILL-LEGACIES

One enduring legacy of the eight years of the Obasanjo administration is the breaking of the Northern Myth. Given the history of leadership in Nigeria, some southerners had come to believe the myth that the north had underdeveloped the south. In fact even some northerners promoted this perception by supporting publicly the belief that leadership was their birthright. I believe that we now all know that with the right kind of pressure, power can change hands. I doubt if power ever shifts. I believe that southerners, especially the Yoruba now understand that misrule is not the sole preserve of the North. In the last eight years, their own son has set a record as the "most disobedient, self-willed leader" ever produced by Nigeria. One used to think that it was just a manner of speech to describe hell as a bottomless pit. Abacha, Nigerians thought had taken Nigeria to the bottom of a political hell. I think we now know better; this hell is bottomless. We need another eight years to complete the full circle of miss-governance. The Ibo need to produce their own *area government*. One can hear them boasting that they will do wonders if put in charge of state resources. The performance of their governors does not exactly make one feel comfortable with this reasoning. Afenifere once led the world to believe that the solution to Nigeria's leadership crisis is a Yoruba man. Let us give the Ibo their chance to loot and reign. Once we have all the major groups in the hall of shame, maybe we can put the ethnic argument to sleep. MASSOB will dissolve once they have an opportunity to lick their hands and clean their mouth. OPC has worked itself from being a pan Yoruba group to a *maiguard* association. Afenifere was once the Yoruba Tiger, now it is merely a *Storming Bingo*. What of the Arewa forum of old men who have suddenly found voice like the traditional dwarf chicken that raises an alarm and disturbs the neighbourhood after farting.

Soon too, it will end up in the pot of soup as every chicken always does. There is nothing money cannot do. I say let us give Ohaneze its own temptation and they will show their true colour. Let Ibos have power to steal as other groups have had and you will see the great Ohaneze dispersal. The historical land hunger that led to the migration of the Ibo may happen again.

18 March, 2007

CHAPTER THIRTY-SIX

APRIL FOOL AND THE MAY JESTER

An old Lion does not roar, it growls because it knows that its time is up and sooner or later it will have to take the back place in the pride. A foolish Lion King waits for a younger Lion to challenge it in a duel and defeat it. If this should happen it is dethroned and beaten up by a couple of other lions wishing to gain respect. We are in the jungle here and respect is gained by brute force. Young Lions are known to roar uncontrollably when they find their voice and discover the fear it instills in all creatures. When an old Lion roars indiscriminately it is often due to the paradox of power. The more power is exercised, the more power is needed. The more power one accumulates, the less benefits of power are available. The less the benefit, the greater need for more power. The ultimate benefit of power is control and respect. There is a curious compensation for the loss of power. Violence and threats of violence are evidence of a loss of control and power. A powerful man does not announce his presence; others make the way for him without him having to utter a word. Animals generally compensate for their lack through various camouflaging strategies.

1 April, 2007

CHAPTER THIRTY-SEVEN

ALHAJI KOKUMO YAR'ADUA

The Nigerian political scene is never without excitement. On Wednesday Nigerians woke up to a strong rumour that the presidential candidate of the PDP, Alhaji Yar Adua had died of some ailment. Most people believed the rumour because of the incident of the previous day at a campaign rally in Lagos. There has been a debate and concern over the health of Mr*Malomo* Yar'Adua. By the way we are talking about the same individual who now appears to be an *Abiku* because of his tendency to reincarnate each time after a rumoured death. Let us look back. Although President Obasanjo has informed Nigerians that Kokumo was cured miraculously of an undisclosed ailment, what happened in the last few days has finally confirmed that the miracle may in fact have been fixed. Or maybe he needs another miracle for a new ailment. Although we are being led to believe that the presidential candidate went on a routine check-up, we know that such a sudden and unannounced trip of such an important person, who is dogged by controversy over his fitness, is at best a gross blunder. The man is ill pure and simple.

We have been asked to challenge him to a game of squash. I will not advise that. Yar Adua's problem with Nigerians is not so much that he is ill. In fact Nigerians sympathize with him. Rumours of his death evoked a lot of pity for his family. One person asked me why the family should continue to pay such a high price for the country. Clearly, many Nigerians love the man but they doubt that he has the stamina to manage the office of the President of Nigeria. A lot of people also believe that the office is not worth the life of another Yar Adua. If I may put it bluntly, many believe that his primary qualification for the office is his ill health. Obasanjo, many believe seeks puppets and fiddles and he has found good candidates in a sick man and an inexperienced deputy. I would like to disagree with this opinion. Which sane man would seek to entrust the business of state to a vegetable?

The modifications of the functions of the office of Chair of BOT of PDP and the sweeping powers to override the serving President in the arrangement shows clearly that we have reasons to believe that in the event of a PDP victory, we will have a surrogate President. President Obasanjo has also confined the Presidential candidate to the back role in the current campaign. He is the one talking most of the time. This again gives credence to the rumour that Yar Adua had actually asked to withdraw but had to stay on because OBJ promised to do the campaigning for him. OBJ is the greatest headache that the PDP presidential duo has. Without him they would have done very well. I think the political opposition is having a field day spreading damaging rumours. Which normal man worth the office of the President of a country will concede to such a demeaning arrangement? Now let us come clean on the health of the PDP presidential candidate. Is he ill? What kind of ailment does he suffer from? Many Nigerians his age are ill of one condition or the other. But we need to avoid a situation where we put in office a man who needs intensive care. If indeed it turns out that we have a candidate who is unfit, I would suggest that the leadership of the PDP should be given a mental examination and thereafter flogged.

Talking about mental health, if Mr President is officially 70 years, I would like to add another 10 years to his age. Or does he have a birth certificate? A lot of things go wrong with the brain at that age. Some of these have early signs that may be confused with resoluteness or bravery. Certain sectors of the brain can go dead leading to hang ups. It may be difficult to tell that this is the case with people who occupy high office because of the compensatory activities of adrenaline addiction due to pressure of office. Once such individuals change to a less demanding routine, you witness rapid decay of brain function. Remember that this is mere speculation and not a science. As a secondary school student, we had a young brilliant man teach us Biology as a volunteer for a week before we realized that he needed psychiatric attention. He was very factual, visionary and with a *kampe* memory, then one day he lost it. With the benefit of hindsight, we realized how stupid we were because we should have known from his loquacity and *koikoi* gaze. There are a few octogenarians in powerful positions in Nigeria. Old men in politics need to be watched closely. In many cases, they are either over the bend or inside a cage.

11 April, 2007

CHAPTER THIRTY-EIGHT

LAUNDRY POLITICS

The conduct of the last local government elections brought to my mind recollections about the history of 419 in Nigeria. It did not start in the 80s as some may believe. That period only marks the massification of the tendency and the professionalization of the practice. Let us look again at another dimension of 419, the fact that like the military and legal profession, it found ethnic bases in some parts of the country. There is always the ethnic dimension to crime and criminality in Nigeria. This arises from a number of sociological factors which make certain individuals and communities more vulnerable. For instance, there are prostitutes everywhere. Prostitution is a human tendency, yet we find that it is more prevalent in some communities, in particular settings and among a social class. Criminality is a potential in all of us, with the right catalyst, a saint can become a devil. Freedom fighter can become a slave master with the right conditions.

As I ponder over the evolution of 419, I remembered the era of rented cows. In those days, it became a practice for people to rent cows and tie at venues of celebration for all the world to see during the day. The impression was thus created that the celebrant was an affluent man, and since the party was judged by the amount of food available, people troop to such venues hoping to make a kill. Unknown to them the cows would have been returned surreptitiously to their owners leaving only one or two. At the party, food is soon exhausted, but no one blames the celebrant but relatives and handlers of the food. He goes away with a great impression as a thick money man. Vehicles are also rented for trips to the village to make good impressions. For many poor people, renting of clothing by urban dwellers visiting the village is an age old practice. Everyone simply wants to make an impression even if it involves a little underhand.

6 January, 2008

CHAPTER THIRTY-NINE

VOTE RIGHT, BE TRUE TO YOURSELF

In a few weeks from today you will all be called to vote in the elections. You are probably now making up your mind who or what to vote for. Some of you will throw away your votes, others will throw in their votes while yet others will cast their votes. It is our hope that most Nigerians will do the latter; but our fear is that, as it is our customary practice the majority will throw away their votes while several will throw in theirs. Then afterward, we all will come together and mourn our misfortune. We will blame the devil and set up praying temples and fast ourselves silly. God will not decide against our will. If you vote for an individual only because he/she is your relative, notwithstanding his poor credentials, you are worse than a lunatic. If you vote in a thief because he/she hails from your ethnic group, do not cry when he/she shares your faith, be ready to bury your children.

As the elections are coming, we are again doing the usual thing which has not paid off. We are again living up behind thieves, we are drumming for wicked people; we are selling our birth rights and mortgaging the future of our children. No miracle will happen if you open your eyes and elect the wrong people because they hail from your ethnic groups; or because they share your faith. Some people cannot just resist joining the winning party even if the devil runs the party. Are you going to vote for your belly or your conscience? Whatever you do, remember when you suffer that you collected your payment up front. When your children die, remember that your vote was your sword with which you killed them. When you fail to get your salaries remember that you took your payment underhand. If you get run over by police escorts, remember to tell your religious leader. Do not be deceived, god will not overrule your will.

Now think! Is it possible for wicked people to rule, if we do not help them? If we cast our vote for the right people and with the right intentions there's no chance that thieves will reign over us! Think right! Act smart! Do not sell your vote. Don't act like a slave. Vote right. There's no miracle about it, we will get the kind of government we vote in. If winning is all you care about when you vote, remember that you may win the election and lose your future. If the highest bidder gets your vote, remember that he is bidding also for your life. The issues are now very clear. Refuse to vote for corrupt people. Who are these people? They are the ones who give and collect Ghana-must-go. They offer you money to vote for them. There are those who have become rich overnight from holding political positions. They pass and repeal laws for money. They steal and protect thieves. They are the assassins. You and I can cause a revolution. All we need to do is vote against a crook. We can have change by throwing out the thieves. God will not act against our will.

16 January, 2008

CHAPTER FORTY

YAR'ADUA WILL NOT CHANGE US, NO ONE CAN

There are certain things a man does for honour. Sometimes we do things for prestige. At other times, it is because we need respect. In each of these the motivation remains that we do it for reasons other than money, even though the primary motivation may still be our own personal fulfilment. In the life of an individual, there ought to come a time when the individual identifies himself within a collective and when he sees his own good within the larger purpose of life, the common good. The motivation for service and performance becomes more than what he or she can get out of a system but how much he or she can put into it. I agree infinitely that each one of us needs some level or the other of motivation. I also agree that reward is an essential component in this. Even more, I believe in equity as a foundational principle for a sustainable system. But we do not have a perfect system, if in fact we can allude to the existence of one in an absolute sense. In a perfect system, everything works. Everything works because all players are perfect. But there is no such system, so men learn how to draw strength from the collective to overcome the limitation of its components. It thus means that the greatest need of our time is for individuals whose primary desire is to work for the emergence of those very ideals which they have identified as lacking in our society.

For the very fact that they have come to identify the problems and have solutions, it means that God has chosen them as His agents to bring those changes into being. God will not write anyone a letter or make a phone call or even send a text message. He has no fixed address so we cannot correspond with Him. He works through the very forces of consciousness and the capacities for understanding and action that all humans have by natural endowment even though differentially articulated. When we come to know the things that are wrong in our system, we have received a divine appointment to find solutions. Whenever we speak with belief that we know the solutions, we have a mandate to implement the solutions. When we fail to do something and whine and complain, we are greater transgressors than those who never stopped to reflect on the implications of their actions. There is a common destiny which we share as humans. There is a journey that we must undertake together as nationals, or members of a group. It is important to recognize that we are nothing without our shared achievements and cannot endure outside the context of our collectivity. We now must focus on the common good and redefine the goals of our lives in this bond of unity. I was once told a story of an elephant that was tied up by a colony of soldier ants. In order to avoid conflicts, they set themselves in groups with each group eating the elephant from different points. They reasoned that it was impossible for them to ever finish consuming the elephant because of its size. They did not think however that the elephant could die. It died within a few days. This is unfortunately our attitude as a nation. Everywhere you go, it is the same spirit of grabbing and eating, hostage taking, blackmail, threats and terror.

This has to stop, don't you think so? Yes, we have a problem of leadership. But I have never come across a system that worked because of the leader who stood by himself alone. In any nation where great strides have been attained, there are great people who put down their great personal garments and joined with others in the muddy terrain of hard, honest work. Who are leaders if not living monuments which have arisen from the fixations of human minds foisted on them by their idolatrous history. Leadership is important but is itself evidence of a people's quality of being. Once in a while a good man with the right mix of character, wisdom and strategy arises to restore the attitudes of his people. But the people must do the work of building their system. Those who are waiting for Yar Adua to change Nigeria may have to wait for Christ's second coming. It is not he that will change us, we must change ourselves.

27 April, 2008

CHAPTER FORTY-ONE

ONE YEAR OF GIANT STRIDES

May 29 has become one of the many public holidays in Nigeria. By the time Yar'Adua is returned by the Supreme Court as validly elected, he would add yet another day for the celebration. Maybe such a day will be known as victory day. In another twenty years, we may be enjoying public holidays for half of the year. Nigerians are now settling down to the fact that judicial victory is not the same as political victory. You may have legal judgement but no justice. Rule of law is not tantamount to a reign of righteousness. Apart from the declaration of the court annulling what was clearly violations of standards and best practices, nothing has changed.

The people's initial enthusiasm has been dampened by the hopelessness of the situation. The apathy and low turnout at subsequent reruns of elections, shows clearly that once again, we have been conquered by the political elite. The godfathers are stronger than ever. The good boys and traditional rulers are getting their reward from the excess crude funds. All over the country, the Governors are doling out consistuency funds, buying cars, executing contracts and celebrating victories. Things are getting better as the song goes and PDP is on the throne for one hundred years. Following the audacious ruling of the election tribunal on the Presidential elections, copycat judgement are anticipated. Worse than this is the "we day kampe" mentality that has followed. Governors whose elections have been annulled and are awaiting pronouncement at the appeal court are busy settling workers, students and political opponents with state funds. In one case, just a few months ago, people were shouting "crucify him, crucify him". The song has changed after the distribution of cars to "things have never been this good"

In one of the Yoruba states, the Governor's name was bastardized in Yoruba language to a "strange or weird dream". Today, he is the "predatory eagle", "the peculiar Governor". In one of the South-South states, workers' salary has been increased. Money is flowing everywhere and foolish people are celebrating their bellies. Nigerians don't care about change or justice. I still am searching for the translations of these terms in local languages. Justice is when we have the upper hand. Change comes when we have the advantage.

For the President, it is heartening to hear that he is "fit and able" to lead Nigeria. I hope also that this means that he is also in charge. One thing is clear that the greatest asset that Mr. President has, is the pervading hatred for Obasanjo. For the one year he has been in office, this hatred has been fed, nourished and used as a diversion. The rule of law, a creative political strategy is now fast becoming "the rule of farce". "The energy emergency" is now truly an emergency. The whole country is in darkness. The eight point agenda, is really turning out to be a pipe dream.

Three months into this administration, it was easy to believe that given the circumstances of his (s)election, the President was being deliberate if not careful. In six months, some people argued that he was warming up and would explode with a bang. Now, after a year of running the engine without motion, it appears as if the fuel is all used up. Promises upon promises, testimonies to his goodness and Nigerians are asking "what is going on here?" I'll tell you a story. The time was 1978. We were preparing for WASC. We were waiting for our Biology teacher and lo, a young man walked in, introduced himself, took out a text by Stone and Cousin and started teaching us some of the most memorable topics of my life. For three weeks, he held us spell bound by his erudition, eloquence, insight, memory work and obscurity. After every class, we clapped for him; his head was hot. Then one day, while teaching about cells, a topic familiar to most of us, he started sounding strange and incoherent. He was obviously "saying jazz" very eloquently. Then suddenly, we realized that our great teacher had something up his head. In less than half hour, we confirmed him mad and bundled him out of the class. Soon after, all kinds of stories about him started to emerge. It was obvious that between us all, there was enough information to prevent the tragedy.

What overcame us? Were we intimidated, careless, amused, disoriented? Madness shows in different ways. The signs for some is loquacity, garrulousness, talkativeness. We may erroneously think of such people as being eloquent. Some may say things beautifully and we applauded them, even though we cannot fathom a whiff of what they said. A dumb man may be mistaken for an introvert, reflective, quiet or thoughtful person. I have known people who have lost it, who for months were thought to be funny until they stripped in public. If a woman is too ill to steal, she may be thought to be a person of integrity. Or if a fearful man does not fight ever, wouldn't we call him a gentleman? The University environment to which I belong, is a hiding place for all kinds of characters. The only other better place will be an asylum. Better because, the inmates have no illusion about why they are there. When a University person is having some wiring problems upstairs, he is called an eccentric. "Lunatic, madness, dementia" are terms that describe non-intellectual, non-elite individuals. If the wires are touching and causing occasional sparks, the person is said to be a radical. Sometimes, the problem affects a fuse and when this happens, one whole circuit may be cut off. The person cannot function where that area of the brain is involved. Such individuals may be thought of as principled. I have seen people who are emotionally unattached, or those who have no capacity for empathy described as being highly principled and disciplined. That's the beauty of our world that a total misfit can attain to the esteemed height of a genius. Let us get our point straight here, there is nothing new about what you are reading here or the condition of our polity. But what best describes it is two unique experiences with traffic. I have found out that at some notorious junctions, when a lunatic or disabled individual controls traffic, there is usually order. But not so with the traffic wardens who are trained and paid for the job. Why is this so? Let's not speculate.

Let us go back to reality. I have tried to take stock of the achievements of the PDP in the last one year. I acknowledge the numerous newspaper advertisements celebrating the construction of boreholes, distribution of grinding machines, the tarring of roads with inflated contracts. These pedestrian and mundane things were issues about two hundred years ago. As we were opening boreholes, the Mars lander touched down.

All our Governors and people of political stature have been to UAE and Europe to hide money. They see what great leaders do. It is not about titles, sex and godfatherism. It is about development and transformation of the human condition. Politics has moved beyond the size of a political party. It is now how much transformation a party can bring about. The time is running out for our politicians and our country too. The night is right around the corner and the biblical thief will soon visit us in our foolishness. Let us look back at the last one year and tell ourselves some bitter truth. Apart from the fact that all those Governors who were clamped in jail are free, what has improved? People can now go about freely, unmolested, to do their duties whether lawful of unlawful. Armed robbers have never had it so good. Godfathers of politics can operate with police protection. Robbers have plundered banks to unprecedented dimensions.

Now, they visit hotels, eateries, drinking joints. I think that we should alot a time frame to robbers when they can operate freely and lawfully since we are also contemplating hiring Niger-Delta gangs to protect oil facilities. If anyone is robbed during this free time, too bad. But at least, we should have safety for the rest of the day. If you are a woman and your husband appears more homely and loving, don't be deceived. He knows that he is safer with you than with his bottle or girlfriend. Nigeria is in darkness, cost of diesel is up dramatically. But for European and Indian hospitals, our President and a good number of our government officials will be dead. They can spend public money to go abroad for treatment but what of the rest Nigerians? Nigeria is a huge graveyard from malaria, maternal death, high infant mortality, robberies and road accident. While our politicians go abroad to blow their nose and buy an analgesic, people die from poverty and disease that can be cured for less than a thousand naira. I would want to agree with those who say that the President is trying. Yes, he is trying hard, just that we can't see what! One area where we thought we would see good progress is the Niger Delta. Unfortunately, we stand the greatest risk of degenerating into anarchy, if the current crisis is not arrested. It is not enough, as we have seen to have a number two man come from the region. The Niger Delta is not like the North where you can have a few individuals "settled" and everyone is calm. You have to "settle" everyone. There is in fact no political Niger Delta; there is no kingdom or race so known and no people so described. It is a geographical collocation. This reality must form the basis of our solution. We are going to fight another war, if we are not careful. But this time, Nigeria will not be victorious. The Niger Delta struggle started as an ideological struggle founded on principles of justice. The first error was to extract the champions, before it could take a nationalistic fervour. Then it was hijacked by merchant rulers who invented youths as military fronts to negotiate their greed. The merchant kings gave way to political patrons who armed and schooled the youths. The emergence of politicians in the scene also led to the factionalisation of the struggle. As the politics got nastier, the youth groups multiplied. The internal crisis in the PDP has further complicated the Niger Delta struggle. There is often no transfer of allegiance to new patrons and patrons have problem putting on leash their youth groups once their aims are achieved.

The current debacle can be ascribed to the fact that there is a mind-set that supports the activities of the youth groups. The proliferation of arms, the acquisition of independent wealth by the groups has meant that they can operate outside the control of their politician-patrons. The new "bigmen" are the gang leaders themselves. Besides, the military invasion of the territory has only complicated the matter by radicalizing the groups and creating a false sense of persecution. This is where the danger lies. The gangs have now become merchants themselves in this complex interplay of trade and politics. They have the arms, they are building international channels and learning new tactics from the global arena. They are no longer the village ruffians but sophisticated terror platforms. They have succeeded essentially in that they have demonstrated (1) ability to strike terror (2) lack of capacity of the Nigerian military (3) ability to recruit. They have also demonstrated to the youths of the area that their business is profitable. As long as this is the case, military solution to the problem will remain an illusion. The greatest problem today is that the struggle has no focus, it has become an end in itself. The rhetoric is now just a means of mobilization. Why is the rest of the country at risk? For many reasons. Kidnapping as an economic and political pressure instrument is now being exported along the Niger to other parts of Nigeria. Arms and ammunitions are now being freely dispersed through the same channels. As long as the crises persists, armed robbery and assassinations will not abate. Let us just wait and see at the next presidential elections. There is one even greater risk arising from a new tendency that will emerge. After money comes power. Soon, the gangs will begin to dream of political power; they will convince themselves that they are freedom fighters. Asari Dokubo, started the elements of this. They will link up with international terror groups. They will identify enemies among other ethnic groups. They will take the fight beyond their environments. Bombs will explode elsewhere. In a bid to retaliate, big ethnic groups will call for military action. This is where the tragedy will begin. Now, let us learn that at this point, when it is so real that there is a chance that a crisis of such a magnitude will occur, the international community will be interested in protecting oil supplies.

The easier solution would be to force a negotiation between the Federal Government and the so called representatives of the Niger Delta for the emergence of whatever turns out to be the demand. If the international community would be forced to take sides, it would be more prudent to stay with the side that will ensure supply of oil, take a position that will justify protection of lives and properties, equity and justice. The Nigerian state has neither a navy nor an airforce. It cannot force the international community to respect its sovereignty. It has an army that cannot subdue a determined opposition in such a difficult terrain. Besides, it is an army that may be willing to bargain – sweet crude is tempting to soldiers who have come to see the value of living to serve their country instead of dieing in service.

1 June, 2008

CHAPTER FORTY-TWO

BRINGING THE PEOPLE TO THE GATEHOUSE OF GOVERNMENT

At 48 years old, we probably are best known as a country that has contributed more clichés to the English Language. Just read the newspapers and you have a feeling that you are reading yesterday's news. Read the speech of a President and you have this sense of de ja uu. You wonder whether you read the speech in your dream or perhaps, someone gave you some hint of what was going to be written. Every government is "assuring" citizens of Nigeria about the "laudable" projects which they will "spare no effort" to execute. Citizens are advised to "tighten" their belts and "make necessary sacrifice" to ensure that Nigeria becomes one of the 20 largest economies by the year 2020. When you add the mystical figure 7 to the rhyming number, you are translated into a magically real world where everything is an illusion. I must confess that I almost believed President Yar'Adua when I read his Independence Speech. Then I remembered that I almost believed Abacha and Babangida. Then I remembered that I narrowly believed Obasanjo. *Na lie*, this time, I promised that I must see changes with my *korokoro* eyes before I believe Yar'Adua.

You know that it occurred to me recently that for the past thirty years, I have been tightening my belt. It all started with Shagari's green revolution, to Babangida's SAP. Does anyone remember STEM – Second Tier Foreign Exchange Market? Does anyone remember the commodity queues under Buhari and Idiagbon. I remember vividly that I had to bathe with soda soap manufactured crudely by the new breed of entrepreneurs. That was the time when adulteration of products, faking and imitation took firm hold. My headaches used to respond to medicine after three weeks of abuse of analgesic. Then I went to the USA and bought analgesic and I was cured in three minutes. It was like magic. But then, I realized that I was a victim of fake drugs. My dad was not so lucky. My mum was nearly unlucky. It is so easy for the President and politicians to ask Nigerians to be patriotic and peaceful. They need us to be quiet to enable them concentrate on their *chopping* spree. Obviously, Nigeria needs a leader. As I watched the financial crisis in America, I was taken aback when I read that Republican Reps voted against their President and put their candidate McCain in electoral jeopardy. I immediately remembered PDP. Bush would either have taken part of the 700 billion dollars to bribe the Reps or the dissenting members would have been expelled from the party. The party, being a cult cannot tolerate dissent. I learnt a new expression from the Americans, i.e. "Toxic loans". Almighty capitalism is getting the test of its life – so soon after the collapse of communism.

The primary struggle that Republicans are having to face is ideological. They may have to accept that the market must sometimes be subjected to the wisdom of human manipulations to save lives and properties. If this bailout plan goes through, a fundamental ideological coup would have been pulled off with great prospect for future directions. Let us come back to Africa, to South Africa where Thabo Mbeki fell to his miscalculations. That's an African President of no mean stature, who is hale and hearty, who bowed to party and the need to sustain peace and stability in his country. In Nigeria, a President is bigger than the country. You dare not talk about his resignation – for it amounts to sedition and threats to national security. The President's misconduct and miss-governance of course has no security implications. Some months ago, I had the good fortune of listening to some top civil servants in a ministry railing against a union and academics for being unpatriotic. This is one of those individuals who become patriots by appointment or election. As he was talking, it occurred to me that he has at least two of his children in foreign universities. From his salaries, there was no way he could afford it. He is not a thief, but he is smart. This guy is simply in the air all the time accumulating estacodes. He attends conferences and workshops organized by rats and lizards for the estacode. Obviously, his wealth of experience has not reflected in his job – just that he has mastered the art of creaming hate words. He is loved by all for his patriotism. Tell me who will desire a change in a country that gives his children free education abroad. Who will not be patriotic if his country feeds his family, fuels his vehicles, flies him abroad for medical check-up and on top of that, pays him an estacode for being sick.

Nigeria can never experience meaningful development as long as the government and people run different economies and live in different nations. If you are a politician or top government functionary, you are not subject to inflation or the vagaries of the economy. This explains why people try as much as possible to remain in position. The lifestyle in government is clearly unsustainable. If we really want change, both the government and the governed must operate in the same market. Government must equalize everyone for those in position to appreciate the difficulties that ordinary Nigerians face. Let us begin by banning government officials from sending their children to foreign schools. Let Government stop overseas treatment for all its officials so that we can all die at home as our patriotic duty. Let everyone buy his own fuel, drive his own car, travel the same roads, drink the same water. Let us ban the importation of generators. Let us all depend on fake drugs and become victims of our hospitals. Apart from armed robbery, it doesn't appear as if there is any other service that is freely available to government officials and ordinary Nigerians. If we cannot bring government to the door step of the people, at least we should take the people to the gatehouse of government. If government cannot provide free education, free health to the people, it should not provide it to itself. What government cannot provide for the people, it should not provide for itself.

12 October, 2008

CHAPTER FORTY-THREE

ADE DE BULL: SUPREME RULER OF AN ARTISAN SOCIO-POLITICAL ECONOMY

In my secondary school days, students were required to take a nick name. In those days we called such names "guy names". The name had to be nasty and mean and you have to live up to it. It was very important that your physical appearance, mannerism and habits match your name. Some of us tried very hard to be recognized. In less than a month, I had disposed of over ten "guy names". I either met with ridicule or the name had no "turk".

A friend found an Indian name for me "mohem", which was supposed to mean "bastard". I modified it and I became known as "Mohem Blast"! I was on top of the world for a week until my thin frame let me down and it was corrupted to Mohem …squito (mosquito). So I lost the edge and respect. There is something about bullies which we need to know. As much as we think that they are tough there is an emptiness which they try to make up for through titles, aliases and violent disposition. The search for respect and recognition is expressed in so many ways that are negative. Now, let us go back to the great guys in our school. These were the big, bullish and nasty individuals. They could do and undo; they huffed and puffed, did booze and drugs. We had names like **iniquity, confusion, dead men**. Everyone tried to live up to their reputation and so they had to invent new ways of being violent. Imagine that if you were asleep and were naked, a rope would be tied to your *abunam* and an alarm would be raised. You can work out the details. A guy falls asleep in the prep, chairs and tables were piled up over him up to the ceiling, all lights are switched off and an alarm is raised. Imagine yourself in that situation. The guys are the ones who also lead the raids into neighbouring farms during lean seasons on campus. They will instruct their disciples to undress so that the juju in the farm would think that they are monkeys. They reason that humans are prone to the effects of juju because they wear clothes. Sometimes, thy walk on all fours into the farms like wild animals. They were really heroes! One thing about this group was that, they almost always failed their school certificate examinations, that is if they do not drop out before then. But with the advent of party politics, many of them have found use for their skills.

On June 12 2008, the city of Ibadan went dead. The previous day, at about 4 p.m., I got a phone call that the strongman of Ibadan politics was no more. Now, we have to celebrate June 11 in Oyo State and June 12 will now be known as June 11 plus 1 – this is the new Math. At 80 years of age, no one would say that the man died prematurely, except of course his PDP beneficiaries. If my father had lived up to 80 years, I would have been most grateful. Yet how we live and what impact are made in our lifetime is not a function of our years. Our impact cannot also be evaluated by the number of paid advertisements, the forced holidays and eulogies of political jobbers. There are things we cannot deny about Alhaji Adedibu, that is that he was in charge of Oyo politics. But we must not intellect too deep about the value of his methods. There is no doubt that he proved very effective but we must not pretend that he was popular by the choice of the people. If we must be very frank with ourselves, there are many who are relieved that an era of politics has come to an end. I have often asked myself how one individual would be so powerful. The answer lies in the political economy of Ibadan and Oyo State. It is an artisan and drivers economy. In control of these economies are NURTW, Artisans, Butchers and Market Unions. These groups have a command structure akin to the military. Their methods are brutish, fetish and violent. Once you take charge you are in charge. What the Alhaji was able to do was to offer the leadership hierarchies political relevance and influence and he in return had their Garrisons at his command. The Nigerian political environment is not built on debates and ideas, it is built on the same parameters under which the great guys in my secondary school operated. What has happened in Oyo State is that we have had an army without a barracks and there has been war without a battle field. In the next couple of weeks, the so called school of politics is going to crumble because there was no school but a group of cowed individuals and others with primordial interest. The market has closed and everyone will now take away his goods. The family should not be under any illusions that things will remain what they used to be. The truth is, loneliness will creep in soon enough. Death is the true test of loyalty, the proof of what we lived for. The regular Amala and Gbegiri eaters would soon discover their folly. Development is not about feeding people everyday on a meal. It is not about gathering the weak together and blowing their minds with false sense of relevance.

Those who truly made a positive impact are the ones whose influence, ideas and relevance continue years after they are gone. But then, we need to ask if those ideas are positive or not. For two decades, a particular approach has dominated the landscape of Oyo polity. And we have all come to understand that foolishness cannot become wisdom simply because people in position say that it is foolish to be wise. The bottom-line for all of us, is if truly our leaders have done well, why are we in this mess?

CHAPTER FORTY-FOUR

DANCING NAKED IN THE STREETS

After the election results were announced I went through Sasa area of Ibadan. I passed in front of the house of a man who was once the most powerful man in Southern Nigeria during the regime of Sanni Abacha. He has become very ordinary and very normal like the rest of us. The once bustling neighborhood is now only a business enclave of pepper and tomatoes merchants. This man was so powerful that with a phone call he made miracles. There were always a couple of cows tied up in front of his house and he gave out cars like pure water sachets. This was before Adedibu made the news in Ibadan. In those days people thought that the Olubadan was a chief under this individual. How time changes. I have had also a lot of time to think of the INEC chair Professor Iwu. Listening to him on T.V. and reading his statements, I have come to see him as a half complete 419. In the face of obvious problems he makes promises he knows he will not keep and gives assurances without evidence. Knowing that this same individual had once claimed to have found a cure for Ebola Virus gave me a lot to worry about. It is either he is deluded or he is demented.

To have an individual like that in such a sensitive position is a testimony to the character of his patrons. He reminds me of the onetime Balogun of traditional medicine in Nigeria who could cure everything under the sun. Before Iwu, there were Ovie Whisky, Humphrey Nwosu, Eme Awa, Ephraim Akpata Michael Ani and Abel Guobadia. For those of them who are still alive I hope they are happy. Many have now been confined to the backwaters of infamy. Will we ever learn? I met one of the former Chief Electoral Officers recently at a wedding. He was alone and lonely. Totally ignored and a shadow of his confined self on TV. Time is a great disciplinarian. The police chiefs of old, where are they today?

Who of them is still relevant in the country? If we can't remember far back in time, at least we remember Tafa Balogun who is now a parable in Nigeria. He was used against the people he swore to protect. Today he is a liability to his family, village and all those who bear the name. Today we see Ehindero going the way of his predecessors. Real power comes from God, not man; neither does it come from the barrels of a gun or a position. We shall see how long all these will last.

I am forced to remember other powerful individuals in politics and government. They are Seriki Sasa, Okadigbo, Umaru Dikko, Adisa Akinloye, Richard Akinjide, Abubakar Alhaji just to name a few. Nothing lasts forever. Let us look at presidents in Africa: Charles Taylor, Kamuzu Banda, Mobutu Sesseko, Idi Amin Dada, Bedel Bokasa, Sergeant Doe, Sanni Abacha, Ibrahim Babangida. These are all powerful men who failed to use power for the people. Where are they today? If decent and humane people are forgotten, what should the wicked leaders expect? Let us not forget those who were once the powerful stalwarts of PDP, who justified impunity because they thought they had power. Today, most of them are either in jail, in court or in opposition. The average Nigerian loses control once he or she is given a desk to sit on. We can do anything to remain relevant. I wonder where Jerry Gana is. He once referred to Obasanjo as the father of modern Nigeria. What a father to have!

I had expected the elections to be rigged massively by the ruling party because the president had said it was going to be a do or die affair, but I did not realize that it will be so brazen. Since 1979, things appear to be getting worse. I think what was different this time was that it was not just a thug affair, Governors and their deputies, ministers, in fact the high and mighty in the society were involved in the field operations once left to thugs. They personally participated in snatching of ballot boxes, thumb printing and disruption of voting. The police as usual provided cover. The reason these individuals got involved directly was because thugs were neutralized by the people's resolve in a number of places. I had been informed that very powerful politicians were all over the place saying that the elections had been fixed. I even heard that they said that nothing will come out of it because Nigerians are ever so docile and that those who lose out will have their expenses refunded to keep them quiet. I think, in this thinking they under estimated the resolve of Nigerians to get rid of fake and useless politicians. I got phone calls and reports from parts of the country describing gory details as people were trying to exercise their mandate. In one instance, the police and thugs of a certain party had dispersed voters with tear gas and were busy thumb printing. In another instance, voting stopped at a polling station after only three people had voted. Voter intimidation was rampant, ballot boxes were burnt, fire arms were freely used and of course lives were lost. I think the greatest loser in all these is President Obasanjo and his team of fixers and of course INEC chair Professor Iwu. He is a total failure and like his predecessors he will be confined to the waste bin of an ignominious history. If Obasanjo has an ear left on his head he will hear Nigerians mourning. There is no celebration in the land. People are weeping and will not be comforted. This injustice is too much. The President by his action has put an end to the fight against corruption and he has ruined the EFCC. In 2003 Nigerians tried to throw out some of the politicians whom the EFCC is trying to get by unconstitutional means today. But they were forced on Nigerians through rigging. Nigerians again have called for change, but the same person who claims to be spearheading reforms and anti-corruption has again frustrated their dreams. What does this man really want from us? One wonders what the defenders of the man are feeling at this time. How are the El Rufai, Nuhu Ribadu, Oby Ezekwesili, Charles Soludo, and others who gave credibility to Obj and his government taking it? This is when their true character will show. In decent societies we would have seen a few resignations. I was secretly hoping that a politician somewhere who was declared a winner will come out to say that he will not accept victory because the contest was not fair and there was too much violence. This would have done more for this country than a thousand boreholes. Can you also imagine a winner saying he was rejecting his victory to honour the dead from violence accompanying the announcement of results? This would have been a more courageous act than would ever be demonstrated by a Garrison. We are not cut out for such greatness.

Our great men and women are petty thieves, robbers, maimers, and murderers. I am waiting for those who spearhead anticorruption in our government, who have become our conscience, to speak and act. I look forward to the day when we will have a police leadership that will stand by the people. I look forward to the day where security personnel will place the country before their personal ambitions. The hands of a man may be tied but for one to act against conscience, truth and equity is a mortal sin. We may be in physical chains but no one can chain a person's spirit except himself. Nigerians should not lose hope. As bad as things look do not feel shame. It is the President and his people who should be ashamed. They are small minds and people of fickle disposition. We need to have faith in the court of law and resist temptations to be violent. Don't believe it when they say that you are weak because you are not violent. It is an act of great courage to restrain yourself in the face of monumental provocation. In the crises that are unfolding, a nation is being born. This nation will be great. Every one of us must take interest in defending our votes at the tribunals. Those who have evidence should be encouraged to come forward. We cannot allow the fraud to stand, but we must also be careful not to lie in filth like them. While we are waiting, do not attend the parties of mandate stealers. Do not be forced to send them congratulations. Express your disgust by wearing a black ribbon. Keep wearing it until justice is perfected. Remember to be found on the side of truth. This means that if your own candidate cheated, please also come out to condemn him or her.

CHAPTER FORTY-FIVE

LET US POSTPONE THE YEAR 2007

I have a very good suggestion and proposal to make to Nigerians in respect of the coming election year. I first made the proposal at the staff club of my University after drowning a double portion of pepper soup. Let me first tell you about this club. I started going to the club after a Nigerian president complained that lecturers don't teach but spend all day at their various clubs drinking and womanizing. I think Nigerians know who can make such a wild statement. He is Mr too know. It is a matter for regret to say the least for anyone to reduce University clubs to such debased levels. At least I know about the club in my University. The liveliest debates on campus take place there. The Foreign relations group of the club is perhaps the only remaining opportunity for consistent and relevant intellectual discourse in any Nigerian University. Of course one must acknowledge that sometimes people get a little excited and discussions can get too animated for obvious reasons. We can blame Guinness and Nigerian Breweries for this. I think that the low point of my club has nothing to do with morals at all. I have met some of the most decent human beings anywhere in the club. It is actually the food that puts me off because I have often wondered if the cooks think we are all drinkers or smokers.

You know after the heat from cigarettes has deadened the tissues of the tongue all food tastes the same. I have had to talk about my club because I first suggested that we postpone or annul next year as a *Soludo*, I mean solution to the crisis of succession in 2007. The open declaration of confrontation by Atiku has suddenly raised the stakes and it is increasingly becoming clear that the year will be a year of many things. If we postpone the year, we will save ourselves the debate over term extension and the attendant crisis. If we annul it, then the year will never come and Mr President can have a life term. One suggestion is that we skip it .The national assembly will not then have to worry at all about elections and other matters associated with 2007, including the budget for the year. The presidency will simply allocate the budget in retrospect to those patriotic elements all over the world. One was quite amazed that some of our legislators were contemplating giving Obasanjo immunity for life as a way of encouraging him to leave office. They seemed to be suggesting that the man is afraid to leave office because of some crimes. *Yeye dey smell for Nigeria.* One of the *yeye* that happened recently was the so called Niger delta stakeholders' forum and the council meeting that followed. Mr President was in his best ever and he has once more put Nigeria on the international hall of notoriety. I saw Lilliputian Governors siring a president that has lost all sense of decorum and restraint. It was a sorry sight to see the Governors shaking like leaves and *buttuing.* I hope that we are learning some lessons from all these. Those who pride themselves as power brokers have so broken Nigeria to pieces that, one wonders if we will ever recover from the current level of crudity. If you have ever listened to the likes of Fayose or his father, Adedibu, you will weep for a nation that has fallen to pieces in the name of politics. The newspapers today are full of threats and warnings by government officials or agents. If the police is not barring its fangs like a dog, customs officials are frowning their faces at Nigerians, or a state governor is threatening to deal ruthlessly with electorates. Constitutional order has collapsed. Governors now equate their pronouncement with laws.

They can announce that people should remain at home and expect that it is a law that must be obeyed. Lawlessness is so deep set that even student unions officials cannot understand why a common member should challenge their authority. Terror and sycophancy are the two major preoccupations of Nigerians today. The country is polarized by a mentality of they versus us, owners, invitees (those invited to come and chop) and slaves; indigenes and settlers. The PDP caucuses are the indigenes and all others are settlers. I sympathize a great deal with Mr. President considering the fact that he left prison and wanted to leave an indelible mark on the sands of Nigeria, but as fate will have it, the sand of shame may very well soil his good intentions. Let us not talk about his achievement here today. They are there for all to see. It all depends on where you belong so don't try to accuse me of any bias. What is clear is that the man loves Nigeria dearly. How else can one explain his readiness to die for Nigeria this time around? I was filled with emotions and came close to tears when I heard that statement. I remembered the harassed and frightened man that Abacha presented on TV. That man has come along way. He has also proved the saying wrong that you cannot teach an old horse a new trick. These are proverbial times when sayings are crashing on their heads. I think you can teach a horse tricks at any age with the right incentives such as extension of tenure. It used to be said that he who laughs last laughs best, but now it is said that it is because he may have caught the joke late. I have tried to counsel those who have insisted that OBJ quits in 2007 to stop riding horses in their dreams. Let us look at the scenario on the ground. Where will he go if he leaves Aso rock? Ota? To do what? Raise chickens? Put yourself in his position with all that has gone on in the last eight years. Let us assume he is clean as far as chopping money is concerned, he will be an unusual president in that respect. If he is really, he has stepped on big toes through his EFCC and disregard for rule of law and procedures.

The man is going to end up in prison one way or the other, if he leaves Aso Rock. The most secure place for him is the villa or as he may have alluded to the land of heroes. We must all learn from Taylor's foolishness. The best protection for a dictator is the place of power. The day you cede power you become vulnerable and no one can guarantee you any protection. Obasanjo's best bet for protection would have been Atiku, if he had managed their relationship well. But since he hates abandoned projects it will be unwise for him to let anyone interrupt his divine mandate. Nigerians should be happy that they fell out. One day both of them may very well share the same cell and have an opportunity to reconcile. If Atiku succeeds him, he is sure going back to his cell. If he has a life term and Atiku fails, a lot of anti-3rd termers should be prepared to beg for forgiveness on TV or run. So beyond simple struggle for power, what we are seeing is a struggle for freedom. Let s assume that the man succeeds in his schemes; we will see the emergence of an emperor. A lot of promises made today will not be fulfilled because he will not need to fulfil them. The sudden love for the Niger Delta will end instead more barracks will be established in the area. Let us end this piece with the current *consoludation exercise*. There is a lot of sense in having bigger banks and we are aware of the reforms going on. I still cannot borrow money without breaking my back and waking up my dead father from the grave. The introduction of 1000 naira is beyond my understanding since it, even now, will encourage people to carry money on them or in their homes. Besides, it is going to make bribery and corruption much easier. One would have thought that a policy that will make cash transactions more cumbersome will promote better banking habits and the realization of a cashless society. This will in turn lead to a reduction in armed robbery. Even reputable organizations are still demanding for cash transactions. The so called online real time banking advertised by some banks is really a fraud. It could be electronic; perhaps online at best but not real time in many cases. Finally, finally, it is curious to find that the organized private sector is actively playing politics of third term. People are forgetting the first rule of business play politics but don't take sides. I hope many will not end up gnashing their teeth and falling down like Humpty Dumpty.

CHAPTER FORTY-SIX

POLITICAL LAUNDRY

I believe that the phrase "money laundry" is a familiar one; but not so political laundry. As new as the term may appear, it is actually in operation in the current political setting. How does it work? It follows the general principle that you could rig an election, after which you all start to argue whether or not the election was free and fair. But once you are sworn in the issue of rigging becomes an academic exercise. You simply settle the most vocal or vociferous elements by asking them to come and chop through some kind of government of national unity. Of course you begin to preach reconciliation, and you know the traditional rulers are readily available to organize meetings to intimidate aggrieved losers to sheathe the sword of bitterness. Those who persist in seeking their right to justice are labelled or threatened in various ways. In fact they are remonstrated to let peace rain in the country. That is not all; prophets are invited to say prayers for the newly elected officials. After much cherished settlement with fat envelopes, they begin to see visions that will divinely consolidate the positions by proclaiming that the occupant of the position is God's agent.

From the way things go in Nigeria, God appears only to support those in the position once they get there no matter how. The various religious leaders have often persuaded Nigerians that no one gets to any position without God's will, whether or not it is by rigging. In Nigeria, it is considered an act of magnanimity, after rigging an election to invite the opposition to come and chop. Otherwise, the winner may just ignore the loser and ensure that neither he, his friends or associates or business organization survived under the dispensation. Since most politicians are actually unemployed and unskilled individuals without any proven career tract, within a short while, they are ruined financially. Their associates jump ship once money stops flowing. The individual eventually has to swallow his pride and beg to be allowed to eat the crumbs meant for the dogs. In Nigeria, government is everything. If you are not in government you are not in politics. If you are not in politics, you are not in business. Everything is interwoven and interlaced. Even the so called private sector is private to the extent that it is an avenue for keeping stolen government funds. In the last ten years, the political terrain has been shifting bit by bit. In 2003 there was massive rigging, more criminal than previous elections in history. But then, the opposition was quickly brought into government in a characteristic spiritual model of compromise. Once involved the opposition was tamed and dismembered more by keeping them occupied with the struggle for loot than by any ingenuity or political astuteness. It is a simple thing to understand if you look at National Geographic or Animal Planet. When you place a carcass before predators, not enough to go round, you ignite a battle of attrition. Once the strong eat up the weak and they tire out through competition, you simply exterminate the last of the gang. The 2007 election has introduced a new game in the political landscape.

Those who planned the rigging were brazen about it thinking that the old model will work. But they failed to reckon with the fact that a lot of people who were hitherto in their camp, who shared their secrets are no longer in their fold. Second fact, too many individuals had built up war chests of funds, enough to finance a war. Government was no longer the sole financier of patronage. The private sector in politics was now equal to the public sector in parity and pound. Having successfully rigged the elections and failed to subdue dissent, the ruling party is now involved in political laundry. First strategy is to isolate the party and the previous government as the perpetrator of the act. This way, it is no longer the beneficiaries of the crime that are in focus, but the so called perpetrators, as if there is a difference between the two.

The concept of the rule of law finds a model in this way. Second, a semblance of disagreement between the past and present is created but without a confrontation. Thus, we see numerous reversals of inconsequential policies. But the foundational principles of inequity and injustice are left unchanged. One way of effecting surface level changes is to ensure that appointed individuals to key offices are those that are not readily viable. So you drop an El Rufai from government but you take up an Alli as an ambassador. In the selection of political appointments, the people are fooled into believing that a break with the past is in the offing, but the truth is that it is a consolidation with the past but a break with traditions. There is an unanticipated dimension to the calculations that has sent those involved to the drawing table. That is the spate of annulment of the elections. The fact that most judges cannot be compromised has left two options. One, confront the legal institution by defying court orders, which will be unsustainable in the long run, or accept the rulings but thwart the judgments. The principle of the rule of law which the current administration has adopted as its guiding framework has a double benefit. It calms down the political fire from the opposition and the international community, while also saving the big political players from the noose of the EFCC. It is akin to eating your cake and having it.

What has happened therefore is a calming of the political storm and settling the political devils. In politics you don't have to be between the devil and the deep sea, you can be above both. While the president was preaching the rule of law and upholding court rulings, his party was busy using the INEC and the police to frustrate the election tribunals. While he was insisting on due process, his party was busy planning to undermine local government elections. We may be faced with a situation where only the President in PDP believes in due process and the rule of law, or where both principles are good political stratagems to gain political foothold. One would like to believe that the president is an honourable man, but one is disturbed that in his party there aren't many of such individuals. In a situation like this, it is only a matter of time before he capitulates or loses control.

There is still a fight ahead. Let us see what is going on presently. Following the conduct of the Local Government Elections, it is clear that no lessons have been learnt from the April elections. From the look of things, it has been landslide all the way, by a party that is so disliked and so depressing. It is a political miracle of greater proportion than the April elections. We have not recovered from the violence of the last elections and here we are again. So what is the calculation? It is simple. Get elected and go to court. At least, you will spend the next one or two years in office while the petition is being heard and appeals are taken. The courts are likely to simply call for fresh elections because INEC will ensure that not enough evidence is available to overturn the elections in favour of an opponent. At the next elections, you rig again and the circle is repeated and so you actually get to spend four years by default. In a situation where service is the reason for politics, this kind of thinking will be considered warped. But in our situation, politics is a business investment from which returns must be immediate. The more civilized of the politicians are involved in political laundry. They are aware that they will lose at the tribunals, so they are investing state funds ahead of time in the rerun. In fact they are already campaigning with state budgets and funding of pork barrel projects. One reason why the LGA elections had to be rigged was to have the foot soldiers on ground to deliver during the rerun.

Political laundry is being done by governors who are working very hard to make good impressions hoping that their capital will favour them over their opponents at the next elections. So you can see heavy budgets from such states, ostensible people oriented projects and recognition of key traditional individuals and principalities. Workers are not left out as largesse are doled out and concessions made. The calculation is that Nigerians are very easy to settle. Fill their bellies and they lose their memories. In fact, people are already saying in some places that such individuals are trying and doing well, suggesting that we should let bygone be bygone. Let us look at the President.

One has heard it said that he will not appeal the judgment of the tribunal if it is against him. If this is true, it does not mean that he will not re-contest. Now, it pays him to engage in political laundry while we wait and to amass political capital towards re-contesting in the event of a nullification of his mandate. If this is so, I think he is doing very well by giving the impression that there is a distance between him and OBJ and a world of distance between him and the PDP. But ask yourself what the evidence of there is, we would only have a bit of fundamentals in the legal arena. Three months ago, the pursuit of due process and rule of law was huge political capital. Today it is losing its potency and efficacy and fast becoming a cliché. Some events have compromised his credibility already. One personality, the Attorney General and Minister of Justice is seen as an agent of his real intention to protect his political backers. The Local elections puts a lot of burden on him which his plea of helplessness cannot obliterate, because, if he had not the parties under his watch, at least not so the police.

CHAPTER FORTY-SEVEN

NUHU RIBADU AND THE POLITICS OF THE BLIND

In the last week or so, the issue of Nuhu Ribadu has re-echoed again. This time it is not in connection with the office of the Attorney General of the Federation. He has been graciously sent on a course at Kuru. Sometime ago, Ribadu was almost a villain because many believed that he was being selective in his anti-corruption crusade. I guess that the current recommendation for him to proceed on course is in an attempt to train him on how to be more equitable in the fight against corruption. One is really amazed that one day, one can be a saint and the very second day a villain. Some of those who accused Ribadu of being selective are crying at the top of their voice to save him from progressing and possibly becoming the Inspector General of Police next year. If Okiro had some political sense, he would have prevented Nuhu from going to Kuru. He will have to pack as soon as the man returns to take up his new appointment.

Don't take me seriously on this, but don't also think it is farfetched. I think that the administration of Yar Adua is fast turning governance to the pursuit of Ribadu and the reversal of Obasanjo's works. Sorry, I am not saying that some of the reversals are not in order, but I think that the government appears on permanent reverse to the extent that one is afraid that the driver may break his neck or run into an obstacle. I am still trying to understand the economic direction of the government now that the rule of law, servant leadership and due process has become household names. After six months, the promise on the Niger Delta has failed woefully. In fact the militants have now exported kidnapping as a model of resource control to other parts of Nigeria. Robberies have assumed a commando dimension, while the roads are in terrible shape. The emergency in the power sector is really turning out to be one of those names that lead to no action. I have heard it said and I think I believe it too that the current administration is very deliberate and the President is a reflective individual. After six months of talk and no action, people now fear that the government may have no ideas and that the man at the helm may in fact be slow. If this is the case as those who refer to him as *baba go slow* claim, we may be heading back to the old order of paralysis.

God forbid that for us. We are all now waiting for the budget, with so much in there for tea parties and entertainment, we are very likely going to see a lot of activities; whether this will lead to progress is a matter for the future. Certainly, the politicians are going to get richer and the poor will pay more for fuel. The anticorruption wars are most likely going to be grounded by due process and plea bargaining to the extent that those who are believed to be thieves will end up the real heroes. We cannot spend the devil's money and fight him. Those who are currently in charge of things are nominees of those we are trying to put in jail. How can that work. What we are going to see are plenty of games but no goals. Let us continue to pray and hope for a great year ahead. As things stand, the indices on ground does not look good for our polity.

CHAPTER FORTY-EIGHT

SATAN ARRIVES HOME

We saw a flash in the sky like a shooting star. Then we heard a loud bang. Everyone thought another plane had crashed. There was an initial hesitation, then a frenzied rush into the bush by many. There was nothing but a clearing and the smell of dung and a creature which looked like a bull on its hind legs but it turned out to be a man. He was handsome but repulsive in an unexplainable way. Transfixed and puzzled, the multitude looked on until the "wereman" spoke or telecommuned with the onlookers. Everyone could swear that he heard a voice, yet no speech was uttered. My name is Lucifer, the one you like to call such names as Satan, the devil and all those terrible names. I have been much maligned and blamed for many things. I am just a creature who likes to let people be and help them to realize self without restraint. I was cast out of heaven millions of years ago, as you would recall the words of Jesus, when he said that He saw Satan fall like a star from heaven. I have been moving through space all this while and I was fortunate to hit earth this morning in your country. You are the lucky ones who have witnessed my arrival.

Since the event above happened, a lot has transpired in the world and Nigeria indeed has seen a lot of excitements. It has been good business for newspapers with the breaking and broken news. There have been things to talk about, little time for boredom or reflection. Life is just one movie and Nigeria a huge screen. The plane crashes and road accidents are just unbelievable! Then of course, politicians have had unlimited opportunities for free airtime. One of them even had to cancel his half year birthday because of a plane crash. Isn't that neat? Can you imagine that all of a sudden, the country's politicians have discovered impeachment? This is just the beginning.

I intend to install real men in all states and make fundamental adjustments in earthly authorities. Expect more excitements. That's life for you, real action! Adedibu will be sworn in as Governor of Oyo state and Igbinedion senior will become Oba of Benin. Ojuku will become the Sultan and Fani Kayode will become the 11th Vice Chancellor of the University of Ibadan. You know what; America will surrender to Bin Laden. Saddam will be freed and adopted as presidential candidate of the Democratic Party. President Obasanjo will leave Aso Rock for a catholic seminary to train to become a *fada*. Don't worry; the land will not be in need of excitement and action. Enjoy yourself. Weep, cry or laugh as you please; only you are not permitted to think or use your head. Follow your belly and be led by your nose. Don't ask questions or resist leadership. Follow the party, follow the leader, stay the course with the president. As long as you fill your pockets, don't allow those rebels get you in trouble. It is not wise to worry about anything or any person but oneself. Akuna matata!

CHAPTER FORTY-NINE

IMPEACHMENT

I deliberately decide sometimes not to comment on so called burning national issues for two reasons. First, there are more important things than the excesses of deluded and infantile rascals who address themselves as politicians. They irritate me. In more enlightened societies, politicians are polite, modest, civil and embodiments of decency. They are not the kind of boastful, indecorous and loquacious brutes that trample on all of us. Everyday I listen and read them, I am infuriated by their threats, display of naked power and disrespect for the very basis of society. I have nothing to learn from people whose existence and influence is based on their propensity to steal and absolute disregard for life. The big time politicians here are either thieves, killers or both. Second, there is nothing new here. Nigeria is a living script of a few mindless individuals. I can mention their names! I am not a prophet, but I am a proffet. It is easy to set the times and the course for this nation.

I am amused by the impeachments and I am not alarmed. I wonder why anyone will be. Why have we suddenly become alarmed that a silly Governor has taken a bit of his own medicine? I have heard people talk about due process, rule of law and respect for the constitution. Are they really serious or are they just trying to impress the Whiteman? Are these people Nigerians? The first impeachment was against the people, the voters, the ordinary Nigerian. Once the elections were rigged, that was it. Who fought for the Nigerian voters? I do not understand it when people talk about justice, when lawyers point to a dead document called the constitution. Isn't it laughable to hear that duly elected officers are impeached? Who elected them? If they were elected, why are the people not fighting for them? What I see in Nigeria is that any impunity can be sustained once you have coercive instruments or are able to buy the court and get a judge to stamp his approval. Is a fraud against the poor just because he does not have the means to challenge it? Is a crime legal because the procedure in a law court provides an escape for the criminal? I am happy to see that Governors are now seeing why laws must be respected. Fayose bribed the house to throw out his deputy. Was the Ekiti house right to throw out the deputy? Governors started a monster that is now devouring them. Each time a speaker rose up in defence of the people, he or she was thrown out. Of course, after a big bribe had been paid. In Oyo state, a governor was removed under questionable circumstances. The judiciary played an ignoble role; just as they have done in Ekiti; Governor Ladoja himself should now know why it is important to obey the courts and respect the rule of law.

When he refused to swear in Local Government chairs from another party, he must have believed that he was a wise man. Judges are just now learning to make it big and everyone is crying foul. So where is justice when judges are bought and sold in the open market? Anambra is a cursed land in Nigeria. The people have played themselves into a cul-de-sac from which they may not emerge in 20 years if they are not careful. The basest of men run their states because they worship wealth and naked power. Oyo state on the other hand is a curious example of a land where princes walk on foot and slaves ride on horseback. It is a land where the noble address petty criminals as their father and promote rascals to royalty. It is a place where treachery is glorified and the strong are raving rogues. People here speak with four tongues and you cannot pin men to their words. Edo is the tragedy of modern Nigeria. It is a land where people are afraid to see so they gouge out their eyes. There is a struggle between two principalities and powers.

The people will remain under subjection for time and times to come. Is there hope for the Niger Delta? Will violence bring development? Who are the men of honour? In this land what one needs are a walking stick and a hat and he becomes a youth or community leader. I f you are violent you are cut for politics. The leaders are the same people who create the problem they pretend to solve. Indolent men are the champions of this place. We created a monster, we deserve the fury.

CHAPTER FIFTY

WILL YAR'ADUA GO?

The Court of Appeal has only recently upheld the judgement of the Election Tribunal in respect of Idris of Kogi State. This situation is sending a lot of shivers down the spine of politicians. It is important for us to reflect on the significance of these judgements and to ponder over the role of the Nigerian Judiciary especially given the crises in Kenya. I am one of those who believe that but for the principled stance of the Judiciary, especially the Supreme Court in restoring hope under the brutish rule of OBJ and his PDP bedfellows, violence, murders and criminality would have become the norm in our land. The risk of mass violence was mitigated by the hope in the Judiciary. So far, we have not been let down and God is on the side of justice. There is now s growing discussion over whether the election of President Yar'Adua would be nullified. There is one agreement, that is to say that the Presidential election was rigged is an understatement.

Nigerians believe that it was a charade and a national shame. That is a matter of semantics. Whether or not an election is nullified is a function of what goes on in the court of law and how those who have the power interpret the evidence before them. There are two sentiments that appear to be recurring among free readers and commentators. The fact is that the honourable justices may decide to uphold the election on account of public good. I will add, that if indeed they want to degenerate to the realm of politics. Who determines public good and by what objective criteria? Can the justices so determine or interpret in their hallowed chambers? Would it not be playing God and being man at the same time? Those who argue that the justices would be constrained by public good point to the time factor and the potential to disrupt the smooth operation of government. That will be plausible if the constitution has not made provision for a line of succession. If a president, his vice and Senate president die in a plane crash, there is still good room for orderly succession. The other sentiment refers to the so-called good works of President Yar'Adua. Some express the hope that he will be allowed to complete his good works even though acknowledging that he was not fairly elected. People fail to see that the problem goes beyond the personality – it pertains to a system, a structure and a consciousness that must be dismantled. A bad tree cannot produce good fruit, not all yellow mangos are ripe to eat. It is not possible to make something out of nothing. For the beneficiary of such a flawed election to be retained by any means will be a travesty of justice. It will send a dangerous signal that once you can hold on long enough and demonstrate some relevance, you can get away with rigging. If a man murders an individual, but goes on to save ten others, would the life of the ten cancel out that of the one? Personally, I think the court should annul the presidential election. Anything short of that would amount to Judicial Laundry of the elections.

There are speculations that President Yar'Adua would not stand for election, should he lose at the appellate court. I hope he doesn't. But if he does seek the mandate of Nigerians, he is quite likely going to get it. That is if the campaign do not reveal more to us about him than we now know. I do not wish for him to run because without him, PDP is doomed forever. The party will certainly lose because of its antecedents and the shameful events of recent memory.

The PDP cannot survive without power at the centre. The party will crumble rapidly and fizzle out into the dustbin of ignominy. I think all attempts would be made to get Yar'Adua to stand election should he lose at the tribunal. Nigerians must wish beyond the personal likeness they have for the man. The biggest sacrifice the man can make is not to run. If he runs, we shall have another three years of the same malady. If he doesn't, we stand a good chance of electing a President with enough moral courage and legitimacy to unearth an ignominious past that many are striving so hard to bury. President Yar'Adua needs preternatural powers to move Nigeria away from the grips of evil that hold her. The best strategy for him, in fact a patriotic duty is for him to hope that the courts will provide him a safe exit. If he chooses to remain God bless him.

CHAPTER FIFTY-ONE

DISCIPLING OBASANJO

I was confused when Obasanjo said that he is commander Adedibu's disciple. Why? Obasanjo being a Baptist Christian and Adedibu a serious Muslim, one could not understand what materials would be in such a "Sunday school" or "Friday tutorial" manual. A disciple is a follower and a servant. So, Obasanjo has clearly declared himself a follower and servant of Adedibu. If an ordinary person made this statement, it would not make the news, but for a former President, to declare himself a follower of violence, a slave of disorder is a bit beyond the sanity threshold. OBJ reminds me of the king's ram with the big brocos which ruled the village with iron horn. All of a sudden, he became tame and timid. The animals began to hold secret meetings in order to find out what was really going on. The tortoise was mandated to approach him for information. "Great one, we wonder what his majesty could be suffering from these many days. The ram kept pointing in the direction of his brokos, but would not speak. A close look revealed a solitary soldier ant that had dug deep and menancingly. "Hey what are you doing there friend" asked the tortoise. "Mind your business, he is my slave". Whoever exposes his big brokos should be ready for the soldier ant.

Let me say here that Alhaji Adedibu's abilities is being underestimated by Nigerians because he has not bothered to acquire honourary academic titles. Imagine if he were to be addressed as Professor or Dr. Lamidi Adedibu OON, GCFR, then his tactics will become the object of study. Because the man also speaks in Yoruba most of the time, many wrongly assume that he is a chronic illiterate. Imagine listening to him on Television, making his arguments in English and throwing in one or two jokes from London. Imagine him in a three piece suit and instead of serving visitors amala and gbegiri, he organizes cocktails and buffet. Would your impression of the man change? Now that the man is the Asipa of Ibadan, the third in rank in Ibadan Land, he has shown to all that he is the proverbial soldier ants that sticks to exposed brokoses. He has two brooks down and who knows which one is next. If God grants him long life, he will one day become the Olubadan and who knows, his son may also be the Governor of Oyo State. This will be perfect power and a pace setting combination.

CHAPTER FIFTY-TWO

RUNNING COMMENTARIES: REBRANDING FAKE DRUGS

It appears that Dr Dora Akunyuli is approaching her new assignment in the Ministry of Information with the same characteristic zeal with which she confronted the Manufacturers of Fake Drugs. We will always remember her and be grateful to her for the way she confronted these heartless merchants of death. In her new job however she needs to take some other lessons from her days at NAFDAC.

Her program of Rebranding Nigeria is assuming the ridiculous. I listened to a statement she sent to a function of Nigerians in Diaspora Organization where she asked for help to counter the negative perception of Nigeria in western media.

Akunyuli is taking after her predecessors by pretending that Nigeria's problems are a media creation. Our problem is not one of perception. Rebranding makes sense, when you have a good product. In NAFDAC, Akunyuli arrested makers and traders in fake Drugs and destroyed the products. I watched a lot of burn fires made of mountains of fake drugs. She sealed up the premises of companies that manufactured drugs of unacceptable quality. That is the spirit. You don't rebrand a fake product, in fact, repackaging may change its appeal, that does not prevent it from doing the same level of damage that it did in the old package. What we call rebranding or repackaging, when it applies to a fake bad products is deceit and mass exploitation. If Akunyuli really wants to help Nigeria, it is to use her position and influence to change how government does business and relate with the governed.

It is not a mere issue of perception that Nigerians live in squalor, that a third of Nigeria's resources is spent between the legislative and the executive arms. It is not an issue of perception to say that our country is a crawling snail.

The Niger Delta crisis is not a media creation. The last election which was ruinously rigged cannot be redressed through mere verbal gymnastics or rhetoric, no matter what name we give it. She needs to understand that the Judiciary has done more for Nigeria in the last two years than the Foreign Affairs and rebranding efforts of all her predecessors put together. When you do the right things the same media will sing your praise. Coming out of a FEC meetings and rambling over issues beautifully is not what Nigerians are interested in.

I think Madam Minister is not acting true to herself. Her zeal is being misdirected towards "image laundry". Nigeria cannot be rebranded where governors and Local Government Officials have so much looted the nation to a stupor. How much rebranding will prevent armed robbers from terrorizing the people. Suppressing sensitive news in the media is not rebranding. It is a silly act of mind control which can only generate rumours and cause greater damage. The style these days is to squeeze the media of advert or patronage for reporting so called negative news about government.

Nigerian government has little to be said about it that is good. Why blame the media? I have a good suggestion about rebranding Nigeria. Let us adopt the cast of Hotel de Jardan in the presidency. I think in this way we can have Chief Ajas as Mr President, Gberegedegbeu as his Vice, Madam Brefa can be in charge of Finance. Chief Udo Okhue is a good candidate for Health Matters and of course, Gbemuan would make an excellent female minister. Dr. Milo Monroe can make a great Communications and Information Minister. Don't you think so, e?

CHAPTER FIFTY-THREE

STRINGING RIBADU

I read with some sense of trepidation information in the nature of propaganda relating to corruption by Mallam Nuhu Ribadu. My worry centres around two things. First is that it would appear that the Police Force itself is working to realize the man's downfall. Second is the terrible disaster which such allegation will become, and its implication for all of us, if indeed it turns out to be true. When I read in the press that police men were fighting over one another to get posting to EFCC, I was not surprised. What was depressing was the subtle implication that it must be because there is corruption in the agency. There is corruption everywhere and in the police particularly, but all of a sudden, there is an attempt to string Ribadu for no other reason that he has stepped on the toes of mighty political patrons. It is common knowledge that the EFCC staffers are better paid than most parastatals. It is also true that police officers fight to get posted to check points and as aides of political appointees. To now single out the rush for EFCC posting is very mischievous. I am not here trying to make excuses for Ribadu. If we are calling for his probe, it is ok if there is something to probe. He should know that his position is a sensitive one and that he ought to be above board in all respect.

What I will not support is trying to finish him up on the alter of political expediency. Ribadu is certainly not the most politically aware individual. He played some bad politics certainly, but he has become the standard for measuring the seriousness of Nigeria in the fight against corruption. To remove him is not the problem, but the circumstances are threatening to rubbish us once more as an unserious people. The timing of his study leave and the statements of the IGP, as well as the court action by the two aggrieved lawyers show that the man is suffering for old sins and political expediencies. I have heard many people say that no individual is indispensable. I believe them. I have also heard it said that the EFCC as an institution is the key operator of the fight and that another individual can perform as well as Ribadu. They may also be right. But from experience, we know that an institution is driven by its leadership and that even in well-established societies, the effect of leadership and personal commitment is often visible. Are we sure that we are at a point when the EFCC can sustain an incompetent leadership? To build an organization to the point where we can talk about it being bigger that individuals we need time and effort by committed and selfless people. One of the things that we all need to learn is that evil still has so much powerful hold on our national institutions and leadership. In fact, some of Ribadu's own mistakes may be ascribed to these forces. It is so easy for good people to be destroyed in Nigeria.

Men of passion don't last in our land. It is either they get destroyed by evil or they are overcome by their passion. No matter who Ribadu is and what he will become, let us remember that those who are today the voices of power were in this land when corruption swallowed us all up. He has done his own bit and it is left for the rest of us to do ours.

I am really wondering if the police leadership and in fact the Government has any idea the level of insecurity which Nigerians experience everyday. While we seem to be making progress in the laundering of our image in the area of the fight against internet scams, advance fee fraud and prosecution of corrupt Governors; we have failed woefully in checking corporate corruption. Instead of the Ribadu phobia that has suddenly gripped the operators of government, we should pay attention to Banks and the Telecom sector where Nigerians are being defrauded with impunity. GSM companies are making so much profit but delivering poor services. This does not appear to matter to the government. It is almost impossible these days to end a call successfully. We continue to pay for poor sound quality, dropped calls and all the shenanigans called GSM. In the political arena, it is palpably clear that we are far from the woods. Rigging is still being done with the help of the police and there is violence everywhere. In the face of all these critical factors, it is a wonder that one Nigerian has consistently been the subject of Government focus.

CHAPTER FIFTY-FOUR

THE GHOST OF ABACHA

Are we still in doubt that Sanni Abacha has resurrected? If anyone is still wondering what is happening in and to Nigeria, I would like to ask him or her to wake up. Abacha is back. In fact we are in the grave yard of evil ambition and the demons and ghosts from the past hunt our land. These are not the days when children should be found on the streets playing carelessly. These are not the days when the aged should walk alone in dark places. The bogey is out on the streets and all must hide in the corners of their abodes or else face the wrath of the devil. You know, my reaction to the crisis confronting our country has gradually transformed from anger to a neurotic amusement, whatever that is. I witnessed once a woman who was supposed to be mourning her dead husband, rolling in hysteria and delirium. She got hold of the man and hit him repeatedly, accusing him of cowardice. She accused the dead man of running away from responsibilities of caring for his family. I am not about to go insane. I think I am experiencing some unexplained psychic amusement because of the disaster that I know awaits the fowler. I take consolation in the words of the scriptures that states that there is a way that seems right unto a man, the end there of is destruction.

The cap is trying to find the head it fits. We are eagerly awaiting the Tony Iredia's NTA to begin in earnest the campaign for Obj's third term in the usually brutal efficacy of the Abacha era. As I look at current developments, I ask myself what Abacha did that we have not experienced even twice as much. Let us take a count of unsolved assassinations. From murder of the Bola Ige, to wasting of Mrs Rimi, the assassinations are so numerous that we need not make a list of them. The common thread running through them is that they are all unsolved. We need now ask ourselves who are the new members of the killer squad. Is the sergeant back? We will have the truth someday as we always do when the hurly burly is done and the battle is lost and won. We will be there to meet with the troublers of our nation. I remember clearly that Abacha tried to tinker with the constitution. He set up an outfit to try managers of failed banks even though he was helping himself to cool cash. That will be his own equivalent of EFCC? It was only after his death that we realized that he was only envious of lesser crooks. Abacha was declared as the only one who was fit to rule Nigeria. All the political parties were going to adopt him as the sole candidate.Today, Mantu's committee is doing an even more effective work. What is left to be done is the million woman march and the Abacha ensemble would have been perfected.

The handling of the current review of the constitution leaves no one in doubt that the intentions of the planners are evil. We blamed General Abdusalami for putting together a constitution which did not reflect the aspiration of Nigerians. We complained that Nigerians had no input in the process. Today we are witnessing the charade of the century. In Osogbo, civil society leaders were arrested and those who were not had their submissions omitted. All over the country, the so called open hearing has become a cult session. It has been reduced to a third term mobilization gathering. Abacha organized the million man march to mobilize support for his self-succession. Today the strategy for succession is the closed open hearing of the SINate. I can remember that the reasons why some people canvassed for the retention of Sanni Abacha for life was that he tamed the naira and was confronting corruption like no other President ever did. It all sounded logical considering the arrests and trial of numerous individuals. Who would have thought that he was worse than his captives? Who believed those who cried that they were being victimized? Then the man died and we all saw his atrocities. He promised to die for Nigeria and he died. The truth however is that he died for *jigijigi*.

Will Abacha die a second time? Time will tell. Under Abacha the courts were under siege. He often evaded court orders. He tried to respect the courts by obeying the orders for a few hours. For instance when the court ask that a person be released, he was actually released and rearrested. But today, no one pays attention to the courts. Even road transport unions and heads of parastatals do not respect the courts anymore. The courts themselves appear not interested in enforcing compliance to its orders. They have also become political in their judgment. They no more give judgment but derail it. Judgments have become so ambiguous that one wonders if the judges seek the input of litigants in their write up. No one ends up guilty and all party go home with something. I guess judges have to settle litigants as well in return for being settled. On the one hand you can be guilty and on the other you are not. Or you can be guilty with reasons. There is confusion in this land.

The political situation in Nigeria reminds me of the story of Nebuchadnezzar and King Herod. Both represent stories of pride and godlessness. When a man loses the ability for self-evaluation, when he needs others to tell him who he is, his end is close indeed. What we are seeing in Nigeria today is not just a case of hypocrisy but a classic case of self-delusion. If we remember, a few years back, the same Obasanjo was the prophet sent to chastise Gowon. He wrote the now famous letter to Babangida on the poor performance of his government. He is the same man who intervened in Togo, Equatorial Guinea and everywhere else where there was trouble in Africa, including Zimbabwe. What a shame to see that the same things he condemned are the ones he is now guilty of. May we not die the death that killed our enemy?

The arguments for the third term agenda are rather perfunctory. Some claim that the president needs time to complete his good works. I don't know if any president ever completes his work let alone the good ones. Even if we agree on the need to do that, what is the guarantee that this good work will be done in the next four years. Even if he could give some guarantee, must he seek to do good by force? We are told that there is none other than the president who is qualified to rule today. This rather ignores the fact of his mortality. "All flesh is like grass. The grass dies and the flower withers". The economic miracle which we hear about is yet to percolate from the books where they are documented to the lives of the majority. I agree that there is a miracle in Abuja. Where else do people become millionaires by doing nothing? In Abuja there is a charm for turning water to fuel and another for converting naira to dollars and pound sterling. It is all too easy to see the misery around the country. Helpless retirees are owed pensions and gratuities, youth unemployment is at an all-time high, people are having to pay for poor services rendered by utility companies, hospitals are ill equipped, and standard of education is poor. Yet in Abuja people still sing that things are getting better. Of course the looter will sing, those who are paid in dollars will sing, those who earn fat pays will sing and they will want the dispensation to continue. But it will not continue because God's judgment upon the wicked will come before the farmer shall return for another cropping.

CHAPTER FIFTY-FIVE

OGUNLEWE'S FALL

Finally the Minister of Works has fallen into ignominy and irrelevance. Transient power puffs up but the wise learns to recognize it and maintains his peace. This is the end of the Tsunami in Lagos I hope with him gone and Olabode George in the eyes of the EFCC hurricane, I hope that Nigerians will learn that there is no alternative to the service of God. Politics in Nigeria is like an assembly of demons. While the devil is happy the demon may think of himself as powerful. But soon he is dropped and left naked to the amusement of those he once tormented. I can't see Ogunlewe's impact on road maintenance. We only see figures on paper. I think the roads are tarred in witches covens.

CHAPTER FIFTY-SIX

THINGS ARE HAPPENING

Things have been happening in the Nigerian scape. The President's daughters are wedding Governors of States, Babangida is making his point on cable in Moments with Mo, some governors are in a frenzy acquiring chieftaincy titles and Atiku is reconciling with Obasanjo. Are all these happenstance, an accident, a coincidence or plain enemy action? Time always reveals the hidden motives of the human mind.

Atiku has gone spiritual. He has now seen the light and is converted. His reconciliation with Obasanjo has drawn a lot of criticisms from people who have failed to appreciate the need to forgive and forget. When politicians reconcile, we must understand the spiritual significance. There is a common pressure, purpose or need. Atiku and Obasanjo alone know what they are about. It would be interesting to know which god was with them at the time of their reconciliation – power, money or 2011. I think both of them know what most Nigerians don't know and would soon know. Babangida also knows. Those who are wedding the daughters of the President may also know. The Governors who are serving their people in the media also know. What we don't know is if we are going to arrive at 2011 before the earth's revolution achieves the date. Time will tell.

Things are really happening. I am still trying to wonder how Akunyuli ended up in Ministry of Lying and Propaganda. This country knows how to rubbish its best citizens. Soon she would be required to lie. She certainly is a strong person and I don't expect her to lie, but just to cover up the truth or not tell it as it is. She has started quite well by seeking to rebrand the Ministry. Her predecessors did the same thing, they repositioned until they were out of tune, refocused until their vision became "half past seven".

I think that the Ministry needs exorcism and rather than Akunyuli paying visits to the Foreign Affairs Ministry, she should do a pilgrimage to Mountain of Fire and Miracles and ask for the help of Dr Olukoya. Power must change hands!

The Global Financial meltdown is really touching lives. For the first time in this country, everyone is losing something. There is now no longer any safe place to hide money. Buy real estate, the value is crashing. Put it in the Bank and you are in trouble. Take it out of Nigeria and you are done for. Invest in stocks and you end up in the stockade. If the meltdown persists for a year, many rich thieves are going to end up as beggars. I am amazed at the way the stocks have fallen. My pension contributions are now in negative returns. The only Bank whose stock value has not changed much is Spring Bank. All others have gone down to meet the Bank at the bottom, in fact some have gone to the abyss.

Now, we cannot deny the fact that Nigeria is not insulated. What is so striking about the financial meltdown is that State Budgets are blowing up. The figures are unbelievably high. It would appear as if our State Governors are expecting a boom – maybe the budgets are a "stimulating package". In some states, traditional rulers are in bitter struggle over who should chair traditional councils. Some are even quarrelling over beads and who should wear them. This country is really a movie theatre of the absurd. How on earth can a person hold a permanent chair over others, some of whom in fact are more competent in modern leadership techniques? One is amazed that we can push history to this ridiculous extent of subjecting a whole people to a so called kingdom which failed even before the grand ancestor of those who are laying claim to supremacy were born. Where does history begin and stop? Some of those who are fighting the anachronism are also bullying others who are seeking the fresh air of aspirations. I think people should become what they want and let every village do what they like with their king. Well, as we know, because so many of the villages are now seeking new opportunities and are promoting their culture and traditional institutions to the limelight, many traditional rulers of large urban communities are no longer satisfied to be addressed as their highnesses. They have become majestic lords of kingdoms of impoverished and disenchanted subjects. Their kingdoms have no access roads, no portable water and good hospitals. Yet they fight over chairs and beads. Shame!

CHAPTER FIFTY-SEVEN

THIS MAN CALLED ANIMAL

I have been ruminating on some titles which will aptly represent OBJ's term as President of the Federal Republic of Nigeria. As one would expect, he would put together his memoirs and of course, he would like to educate us and advise the next President on the strategies and tactics of governance and democracy. What would best represent his legacies? In his first life, he wrote *This Animal called Man; My Command; Not My Will.* This time around we expect him to put the following together: *Do or Die Politics* and *This Man Called Animal.* His beloved student politician, ex Ford Foundation expert, ex adviser, failed PDP Governorship aspirant and supervisor of PDP campaign in Edo, Professor Ihonvbere will gladly put together the Do or Die Politics in Nigeria. The other title should be a Biography. Only the man should write it.

For one reason, a lot of what will go into it will be one man's interpretation of the facts. I would like to think that in his heart of hearts, OBJ knows clearly that he has not ended well. If anything he should be a very sad individual because the last elections have shown most clearly that he could have made a great leader in the 14th century. I have always believed that it is not too important how a leader starts, how he ends shows more about the real person than tons of books written about him could possibly reveal. The character of a man is best revealed when he is under pressure not when everything is going well for him. A law abiding person is not the one who obeys laws under normal situations, but one who stays with it even when he has everything to lose thereby. One of the tragedies we have continued to live with is that we have never as a people had the opportunity to choose a leader for ourselves. A couple of people have consistently given us mean and selfish individuals to mock us and wreck the future of our children. The last Jamb examination showed clearly that our people have learnt quite a lot from Mr. President and the PDP. People now talk about rigging examinations not just cheating. I saw people clustering in places, solving questions and sending answers with mobile phones. Individual cheating is giving way to group effort. I am sure that Ribadu will be very happy about this. Our young people are so unfortunate to say the least. We have always celebrated cheats and rogues in Nigeria. Even the good people are at best wicked men in many cases. I do not want to mention names here hoping that there will be opportunities for some of our leaders to reform. But I must say that our traditional rulers are fast becoming a curse to our people. To think that some palaces were used to compromise the elections was to me an ancestral disgrace. I thought that they will be satisfied with the frequent raises in salaries, new cars and bribes they collect from Governors and LGA chairmen when their subjects are languishing in abject poverty. They once more re-enact the slave trade.

There is a certain traditional ruler in the South West who has given titles to all the notorious thieves and liars of our time. I wonder how people still manage to prostrate to greet him. Nigerians are trying desperately to cope with the heartbreak that followed the elections. Some people have concluded that we are a very docile people. I do not think so. I just think that we are just more civilized than those who rule us. The common man is a better person than the so called educated elite. Many of us are schooled but not educated. Others are educated but not cultured or enlightened. Even among the enlightened not many are wise. I am very happy that the violence following the election did not meet the expectations of those who wished to extend their tenure. What many did not know was that some quarters anticipated chaos at a scale that would have made an emergency inevitable.

Unfortunately for them Nigerians and particularly the contestants chose the part of law and order. The government has not said that the elections were ok, what they have said is that it was freely, fairly and transparently rigged. But international observers dispute this. They state that what we had was not even rigging, but that there was no election at all. So the talk of human imperfection that was the defence of OBJ does not arise. Human systems are imperfect and election malpractices occur everywhere, but humans also have standards against which we measure behaviour. Ours had no basis at all for comparison. Although some electoral thieves are under the illusion that they will keep their loot, Nigerians should be patient with the courts. In the past, after elections people go about on thank you visits. Today however, our winners go to thank INEC and Maurice Iwu. There is so much said and written about the INEC chair that I believe may not be true. For instance, how can a man attain the level of a Professor without ever having a first degree? He must be a genius! Obviously from his handling of the elections he is not. I think that people have a problem spelling his name in their haste to find negative information about him.

If you request information about EWU instead of Iwu, what do you expect to get? There are a lot of anecdotes flying around these days as Nigerians try to cope with the international humiliation visited on them by their president. One goes thus: **What do you expect from an OBJ exam? Answer: Cheating!** The EFCC has become Electoral Fraud and Cheating Commission and the name of the head of the agency is now *Ribadun*, ie. Bribery is sweet. The current beneficiary of the grand theft of an election has been touted as an intellectual, a great mind, a performer, a man of integrity. Are we really speaking the truth about him or are we again hoping to benefit from his administration if he can sustain the fraud? How can a man who benefits from fraud have integrity? He has praised INEC for a job well done contrary to the belief of most rational people. What do we know about him really? What has he promised

Nigerians? What can we hold him accountable for? Our elites are at it again. The Vice President (s)Elect has just been to a leadership course in Harvard according to some sources. I believe he is just trying to learn from our bankers and technocrats who attend two day babysitting workshops in the US and mislead people into believing that they were born and bred in some American University. Inferiority shows up in many ways. I want to sign off by stating clearly that OBJ will yet be the greatest loser of our time. Providence gave him the rarest opportunity to be an exceptional world leader, but he squandered the opportunity out of vindictiveness, short-sighted ambition, failure of character, indiscipline, greed and lack of humility. OBJ was neither a philosopher nor an ideologue nor a believer nor an intellectual nor a wise man. Now we are going to have at the helm of affairs a reluctant person, who we know little, or nothing about; most likely without a plan and who has made no promises. God save Nigeria! One quick advice to him on dealing with security. Follow your predecessors plan. Marry many women, have many children, plant them in sensitive places. Better still, inherit this legacy from your predecessor.

Francis Egbokhare

CHAPTER FIFTY-EIGHT

OSHIOMOLE, WILL EDO RISE AGAIN

Edo State has become like dead dry bones. Years of misrule has ensured that a state that was once the envy of Nigeria has become a political aside, a social exclamation and an economic cripple in the nation. I remember as a youth, that other Nigerians would introduce themselves as Bendelites and join us in speaking pidgin in order to woo and win the heart of girls. As a manner of speaking, Bendel reigned and ruled in Nigeria for many decades. We were very proud and confident people. I remember vividly that old Bendel dominated sports until Oluyole 79 when Oyo State swung victory to Lagos by many means more than fair play. Bendel effect led to the spread of Nigerian Pidgin to all nooks and crannies of the country. Today, it is the most widely spoken language in Nigeria. These were the days before the creation of States. Following the creation of States and the emergence of the politics of misfits and nitwits, the glory of a once thriving culture and civilization was consumed by greedy and half-educated entities of hardly human propensities. Let me say clearly, that Ogbemudia was the only real Governor we have had. He too, though has become one of the many willing victims of a deluded politics and warped power arrangement. Professor Alli made his impact; but I can hardly point to any one after him. In over two decades, the Edo and Delta States have been held hostage by those who at best could have served in Village Councils.

Edo State has had the misfortune of one tragedy after another in politics and administration to the extent that in the South-South arrangement it is not even a factor. I am amazed when I see pictures of the honourable men and women. I am often of the impression that the house is a costume party. When you listen to those who represent the State, you wonder how we ended up where we are. The politics of Edo has long been in the hands of *NURTW*. They are the wise men. The administration is a struggle between cults and violent groups of all shades. The victory of Comrade Adams Oshiomole at the courts has once again rekindled the hope of a conquered people. People may not know that Adam's political constituency and his origins could not have given him victory but for the fact that Edo people put their differences apart to elect an individual whom they believed had the capacity to reinvent the state and restore hope. Adams won the elections. The court has reaffirmed the will of the people and it is a resounding one. Now Adams will have to live with a new reality outside what he has been familiar with. Politics is not Unionism.

There are two realities and many expectations. He has to choose between the short term; between personal sacrifice and convenience; between service and power; between his party and the people and between submission to royalties, godfathers and the masses. I was not at his inauguration. But it was easy to see from T.V. footages that the hawks were all around the meat once again. In due course, we shall see whose victory was celebrated at the Samuel Ogbemudia Stadium, whether it is the people's, Oshiomole's or his sponsors. There are those elements in Edo State who cannot be persuaded to change their ways – they will surely demand for payback. We shall soon know the level of the Governor's commitment to democracy, when he organizes his first election. I must say that all over, including Lagos, we have yet to see a party that is committed to fair play. Those who would make deep and lasting sacrifices must be willing to risk their own power and position in the interest of the people. As I congratulate the people of my beloved Edo State, and "The Governor", I wish to ask them to join hands in uprooting the menace of secret cults and violent politics. "The Governor" must address poverty and access to qualitative education. The methods and processes of governance must be restructured radically to institutionalize integrity and involve the masses in the process of governance. A sincere and accountable administration can achieve a lot in a short time. But a misguided one can do nothing even in a life time. I would like to suggest that "Village Governments" be constituted and be given roles not only in governance but also in budgeting and monitoring of the operation of all aspects of service. Edo State has an advantage over many others in that you do not need to persuade people to go to school. But people must be assisted in creative and innovative ways in delivering qualitative education. One way to accomplish this is by harnessing technology and human capacities creatively to balance the iron triangle of cost, access and quality. It is not always true that quality must be expensive. In fact, most times it is expensive because the greater part of the funds are used to service patronage of politicians and greed of civil servants. Edo State has a crop of highly educated and skilled individuals who can be mobilized to serve. Many will be willing if "The Governor" can rise above power play and crass politics.

The politics of Edo is by gun and thugs and many decent individuals would not like to be subjected to the rule of godfathers and Agbero. Edo also has a crop of wealthy individuals who can invest in the state. "The Governor" has to demonstrate integrity and seriousness to get them to serve the state. The tone of governance will do more to influence change and mobilize people than rhetoric and titles, appellations and branding. He should not just talk but act.

I would like to commend Comrade Adams Oshiomole for his doggedness in fighting through the elections petitions. I want to say that there are many who are looking up to him. There is great darkness in the polity. Blind men and women are striding arrogantly in Nigerian polity. In a world of great light, elites in Nigeria are fighting hard to gouge out their own eyes in order to become accepted in this politics of the blind. I hope that Oshiomole would join Governor Fashola of Lagos to say "we can". His Government must deemphasize opulence in his style. He must live as a normal person and identify with the people's poverty. His economy must be the people's economy. He and his cabinet cannot be "jeeping" about and oppressing the people with sirenes and horse whip as is the normal practice. Soon, he may develop "fat neck disease" and "rosy cheek syndrome". He should remember the blood and sacrifice of those who fought to see his day. Soon, people will be grovelling and seeking to carry him into his bedroom, he should not forget the feet that walk the streets bare. Soon, he will hardly hear those around him differing from him in any way. He will be his excellency and be excellent even in wrong doing. He should remember the fate of those before him. As for me, I ask, will Edo rise again?

16 November, 2008

CHAPTER FIFTY-NINE

ARE YOU THE ONE WE ARE EXPECTING?

2008 is gone for ever. That year, like all other years had its ups and downs. Significantly the high points were the fritz generated by Obama's victory in the United States and the emergence of Adams Oshimole as Governor of Edo State. Too many things went wrong in 2008. As usual, Nigeria wasted the opportunities created by the unprecedented rise in the cost of crude oil in the global market.

Today, the predominating issue is the global financial meltdown and the recession in the world economy. In 2008, Jos boiled over once more. It stills beats my imagination how a local Government election can become grounds for ethno religious violence. While the Mumbai bombings was drawing outrage of the world, greater carnage was taking place in Jos with little more than a passing notice. Nigeria needs to know that it no longer really counts in world affairs. In the last quarter of 2008, Ibadan and other south west cities were taken over by robbers. Their primary targets were banks. It was so disgraceful how these robbers took over Ibadan with little resistance from the police while this was going on the Police establishment was busy hounding Ribadu. There is a bit of a respite now that OPC have taken over guard duties in Banks. After several months of waiting, President Yar Adua finally reconstituted his executive council. It is over a year now since he dissolved Councils of Universities. His seven point agenda continues to be a figment of some imagination. His vision 20:2020 has remained a mantra. We still don't know his state of health. I am reminded of Nero who was fiddling while Rome was burning. The global financial meltdown and the crash in the price of crude oil will determine a lot of what to expect in 2009. Primarily, the Laissez fair market capitalism has collapsed even though not in the same symbolic drama experienced with the collapse of Soviet Union, the Berlin wall and socialism. It is a subtle dismantling of ideology as is the case with the modern Chinese experience where political communism cohabits with economic capitalism. You may call it Asian pragmatism. Nothing new came out of Africa in 2008. Just the same old story of failure, disease, dictatorship and poverty. Congo is still boiling. Zimbabwe is seething. South Africa is band to unravel within ten years. Nigeria is failing gradually. 2009 will make or mar the politics. If oil falls below sustainable levels the era of delay in the payment of salaries will come back.

Labour agitations will be abundant. Power supply will collapse. There will not be enough to share by politicians and so we shall witness political upheavals. The reality of the economic meltdown will become obvious by March. If our Banks don't fail, it will be a miracle. As I look at 2009, I am tempted to despair, but I will not. I am made for adversity. I remember that I have survived greater challenges and more turbulent times. From post-civil war hunger, through SAP, WAI queue to the manipulative exploitation of IBB to the repressive era of Abacha, I have lived by my wit. Life has never been easy. I am part of a generation that this nation has offered nothing but promises, lies and deceit. Am I bitter? No, not at all. I am only now ready to stand up and fight. I am prepared to challenge those who plunder the nation and dispense poverty in the land like pure water. What this hardship has done to me is that it has cured one of ethnicity and removed religious bigotry, from my elements. We all can see that bad leadership is not a Northern disease, it is a national malaise. From the Babangida of this world to Obasanjo, we have seen that every ethnic group can produce a tyrant. Nigeria has what it takes to make a devil of a saint. Our country is built upon falsehood and we need to confront it as its foundation. Both Christian leaders and Muslim leaders have failed Nigeria. Failure has no religion. Sin has no language or colour, it has no gender. This country has taught me not to hate, because the greatest injustice I have received has been by the hands of my own kit and kin. There are some who believe that the Salvation of Nigeria will come through prayers. They need to pray hard. It will come much faster and their prayers will be heard much deeper if they who pray will extricate themselves from the corruption in the land. The greatest power against change in Nigeria is that most of us are really not for change but advantage. We want to take charge and control things. We want our kit and kin to exercise dominance and power. We are in a rat race for advantage. The grim reality is that when it comes to corruption, there is no masses. When it comes to the love of money, there is no religion. That's why, God will not hear us. Who will He destroy for the other? I think we most begin by striving to be different. Those who recognize that there is a problem have a divine call to fix it. The starting point is to avoid being part of the problem. Nigeria needs positively crazy individuals. It doesn't require too much, just ensure that you are an example where you work. You will certainly win a disciple. This is how to raise the critical mass, until what you stand for reaches the tipping point. If you still collect bribes where you work, fail to do your work diligently, benefit from undue advantage, you have no grounds to complain. Nigeria will change when we hate the status quo enough to feel a personal need to do something. If our teachers would do their work diligently, half of the crisis in the education sector will be solved. If the medical doctors will uphold the Hippocratic oath, medical practice will be radicalized. If we all strive to earn our pay, the land will be transformed. We are too busy praying for solutions to a problem that lies at our door step. When I visit any establishment in Nigeria, I see dead men not workers. The average Nigeria worker is as guilty of fraud as the corrupt politician. The police complain that they do not have sophisticated guns as if they need mortar to kill. Lecturers complain of lack of modern equipment as if that explains why they fail to go to class. Students say that they have no access to modern books as if they have read the old ones. If we refocus and use what we have, we can get what we need. It must all begin with us, who we are, a reflection on where we missed it. Gadgets and equipment never transformed any land, people do. We are the reason why we fail. As we start the new year, we need to be creative in positive things. We need to find out how we can make a difference and be ready to pay the price for it. We all want to succeed and there is nothing wrong with that, but not at the expense of someone else. We can still succeed without jeopardizing the future of another individual. I like the end of a year because it provides one time to stop and reflect. The beginning of a year gives one a new opportunity to strategize and refocus. I wake up feeling renewed and powerful at the beginning of a new year. Can you imagine if we go into everyday with as much expectations as we go into the new year? Imagine waking up everyday with the kind of hope that launched one into the new year. What great achievements would we attain if we go into everyday with the same levels of faith, same degree of energy, fervour, warmth and power of prayers that propelled us into the new year. The renewal associated with the birth of a new year is a great source of power that we can latch on to to transform our lives from the bland repetition and routine of failure. We can tap the momentum generated by the new year to address some fundamental shortcoming of our life. The good feeling, that comes at the dawn of the year holds potentials for extraordinary achievements if we can keep the momentum. The trick is to recreate this often enough so that our life becomes one big flow of positive energy. If we can make everyday a new year, every month end a refreshing moment, we can turn the earth around and keep the sun from going down. Make a point of being a great person this year. Set your heart upon great achievements. Extend the barriers and limitations of small thinking and beastly consumption. Refuse to be dragged into the crowd of the dead alive. Don't fall for the arguments of error and self-interest. It is so much sweeter to serve and be useful to others than to wallow in selfishness. It is a happier life to live and a richer experience to be the reason why things work and lives are changed. Welcome to 2009!

CHAPTER SIXTY

24 HOURS AS A POLITICIAN: AVOIDING THE WEB OF A TARANTULA

There is a time in one's life when one is so eager to make a difference and feels so dissatisfied with the status quo that he feels he can die for a cause. Somehow, I have the feeling that if one is truly convinced beyond reasonable doubt that he will die, he is likely going to prefer to live to fight another day. That is the guerrilla philosophy and approach to the struggle. You may not accept this line of reasoning if you are a suicide bomber or one of those bearded radicals. If you are especially eloquent, you may in fact be in love with your own voice to the extent that you become your own disciple. Be careful when people call you a radical. You need to be sure that you are not just a rascal searching for a cause, or a disgruntled person looking for opportunity. It is important always to weigh the causes for which we want to lay down our lives. More importantly do we have to, or is it our life that is really the issue? Or is our life actually worth the cause or is the cause worth our life? Let us ask ourselves some fundamental questions. If you knew that Nigeria would never make it, would you continue to labour for her; and fight for good causes? If you found out that there is no after life, and that life adds up to nothing would you wish to be martyred for what you believe?

The unknown and the known uncertainty drive men to make commitments with doubtful value. Even the best of intentions should be scrutinized because in it, we may be puzzled to discover the worst kind of selfishness. If we look beyond the material level of reward, and if we are willing to accept other forms of currencies to transact human needs, you may find that sometimes, the thief, the murderer, the slot, the base are simply the less sophisticated in the game of guile which humans have promoted to high culture. Who is the prostitute? The lady who sells pleasure for money, or the one who sleeps around for pleasure and high company; the house wife who extorts money from her husband to permit him his conjugal rights? Who is a thief? The one who appropriates your property by force of arms, deceit, or the one who achieves same result but makes you feel good about it. Who is guilty of a crime? One who hatches it or one who lacks the courage to follow through? The distance between most people who claim to be clean and their criminal counterpart is either courage , the lack of it or foolishness. Sometimes it is just a matter of nomenclature. Whether you say that a man was killed, assassinated, murdered or kicked the bucket, we all know that the grave is the end of it all. A carcass, remains, corpse, etc all refer to dead body. I would like to tell you a story of a particular 24 hours in my life when I was a politician. This day, I was to be the Deputy Governorship candidate of one of the two other viable parties, not the PDP. Afriend recommended me to the Governorship candidate. After the initial phone call, we struck the right cord, or so it seemed. I was curious though whether he saw me as a good tool for his majestic convenience. Eventually, we were to meet on this day in Benin. I think now that as a Professor, I must have met his criteria of a compound sucker. My sister was getting married and I arrange to take time off to assess things for myself. I arrived at the party secretariat, a very bare office with scruffy looking assistants, nothing inspiring, all too much of nothing. The candidate arrived in style. He had all the airs of a prince in waiting. Mobile police guards, jeepy convoy, you know the typical successful Nigerian politician image—all hot air and big garbs over a scare crow. I asked to know why the ferocious guards and the guns. He assured me that I will soon be allocated my own guards once I am unveiled as the assistant big man. Truly, I was really keen about serving my people, but not as a prisoner of political parties or organized mobs. W e went in search of one of the party stalwart who is a former Governor. He was not home but I could see his palacially sinful abode. Then, I was told that I had to fly to Abuja the following morning to obtain the INEC forms, then I was to make the false claim that I joined the party two years earlier. Although, I had been led to believe that the election expenses was to be covered from some source, the big man wanted to know how much I had to cover the Abuja trip.

The lie was for me evidence of wahala in the pot. Of course many more lies will follow to make the first one work. The thought of missing my sister's wedding was heavy in my heart. I am her father as a matter of fact. Would I ruin one sure heart to gain millions of uncertain attention? I was sick with conscience and there and then I wanted out. Don't also forget that the current Governor of Edo State was in the race and for most Edo people; he was the saviour they were waiting for. I was a political stratagem, a pun for negotiation. I can't explain here how that was to play out, but I will tell you that it was a mind brilliant by half that was at work. The problem was that he had a deputy who did not have the right fire to drive his illusion. Elections in Nigeria are not a contest of ideas. My elder brother made this point clearly. I used the excuse that I was going to consult my siblings to free myself from the hole into which I was being nudged. My elder brother asked me a defining question; ''if you are given a cutlass to behead someone in the name of elections would you?'' The answer was obvious. Then he said ''it is not yet time for your kind; elections here are won by guns and thugs, you are too decent.'' I switched off my phone for the next one week. One or two of my siblings thought I should give it a try. They were just being innocent. Even if I wanted to play politics, certainly not as a Deputy Governor. In the current dispensation, they are glorified house help. I am too independent minded to be confined to a political boys quarter. No need to kid myself. Later when I related this story to some of my acquaintances, they thought that it was an opportunity to serve. Remember the usual argument that if good people don't get involved in politics, they should not complain when bad people are wrecking everything. This good man, if I am truly one is not a stupid good man. Events following the elections vindicated me. The Governorship candidate ran away from Nigeria. Of course, the election was followed with litigations and today we can all see the outcome. I am sure that Oshiomole would have preferred to be Governor in a less compromising circumstance. I am ashamed that we do not appear to learn from our failures. But you don't go and eat poison because you do not want to be seen as unpolished or rude. Many Nigerians are frustrated with the insensitivity and recklessness of our political elite. This notwithstanding, accepting to compete as Deputy Governor would have amounted to ''eating witchcraft just so you live up to peoples' perception of you or your reputation. I think that any reasonable person going into politics wants to make a difference, but how possible is this without a platform or authority? As far as Nigeria is concerned, there is no political party with any ideology. Any change, if it happens will be an accident; any individual who performs would just be an aberration. The kind of politics that we need is one that is built on ideology. So, what is important in life is not all the great ideas one has or the zeal or passion to make a difference, one needs a platform and a critical mass of like mind. A foolish man who is pragmatic has more hope than ten wise men who fail to see beyond themselves. So it was that I switched off my phone for days. So it was that the elections were freely and fairly rigged. How glad I was that I avoided the web of the Tarantula.

CHAPTER SIXTY-ONE

FIGHTING RIGGING AND VIOLENCE WITH BIOLOGICAL WEAPONS

Nigerians are very imaginative. I was told of the story of how some individuals in one of the South West state dispersed thugs who were trying to rig an election. In this era of biological warfare it is no longer necessary to carry arms and ammunition. The police may also consider deploying some of these modern instruments of violence. The story was told that some thugs had gathered with guns and machete to disrupt voting and forcefully carry away ballot boxes. Desperate members of the opposition quickly assembled and obtained the services of a snake charmer. As they were approaching the polling area, the henchmen were bracing for the imminent show down with the power of the law as a backup just in case of "incasity". They did not at all bargain for what happened next. The charmer brought out his snakes and threw them at the big guys. Within a few seconds, the whole arena was clear and clean. Some even left their shoes behind. Snakes are mightier than the gun and the cutlass. Bees and scorpions are also good weapons of mass dispersal. I recommend that the police should spend some good money to hire bees for riot and crowd control. The good thing about them is that they do not discriminate. During religious riots, use bees. The casualty figure will be very low but it will have more effect than guns. Scorpions will be extremely good if they are dropped from the sky. *Werepe* is a good weapon, better than tear gas, water and acid. In order to control politicians in the coming elections, the police should consider announcing that it will use any means at its disposal to enforce the law, including snakes, bees and scorpions.

GLOSSARY

A

Abacha: A former Nigerian Head of state

Abiku: A child in Yoruba mythology who reincarnates and dies repeatedly

Abunam – euphemism for male genitals

Acting Bigman of Obododike: meaningless titular reference for vanity

Adedibu: Political strongman in Ibadan

Afenifere: A Yoruba socio-political group

Agba iya: Yoruba for dishonourable old fellow

Agbo-jedi – prophylactic for all kinds of conditions that are medically unproven – most commonly used to treat pile and sexual dysfunction associated with excessive consumption of sugar

Ahmed Sanni: A former Governor of Zamfara State

Ajebajepanu: A derogatory Yoruba term for people from the Midwest Nigeria.

Ajokuta maamomi: A derogatory Yoruba term for people from the Midwest Nigeria. It means people who eat without drinking water

Akpata Ephraim: A former Chair of Electoral Commission in Nigeria

Akwa Ibom: A state in South South, Nigeria

Alaafin: King of Oyo City in Oyo State of Nigeria

Amala: A Yoruba meal like semovita mad from Yam flour

Ani Michael: A former Chair of Electoral Commission in Nigeria

B

Babaism: A mockery of philosophy associated with President Obasanjo

Baba Iyabo: Nick name for former President Obasanjo

Babangida: One of Nigeria's military Heads of State

Balogun: A Yoruba title for a warlord

Bendel Chop chop: Pidgin for indiscriminate eating

Bida in Niger State of Nigeria

Bini: Benin

Bukataria: Local eatery

Bunbun: buttock

Bush meat: Venison, also derogatory term for mistress

C

Calabar: An Efik city and capital of Cross River State in Nigeria

Cotonu: Capital of Republic of Benin

D

Democrazy: A corruption of democracy

E

Eba: Cassava granules prepared as semolina

Ebira: A language and people of Kogi State of Nigeria

Edoid: A language group which includes the language of Benin people of Nigeria   Igbinedion: A former Governor of Edo State of Nigeria

Ehindero: A former Inspector General of Police in Nigeria

Ekaladerhan: A prince in some Benin mythology who became Oduduwa in Ife

Ekiadolor: A village in Benin area, Nigeria

Ekiti: A state in South West Nigeria and Yoruba sub-ethnic group

Eme Awa: A former Chair of Electoral Commission in Nigeria

Eranko: Yoruba for wild animal

Ewedu: vegetable leaf and drawy sauce made from it

F

Fasawe: A friend of President Obasanjo

Fixitism: Political manipulation and predetermining the results of an election.

G

Garri: granules or semolina made from cassava and eaten as food

Gbegiri: Bean soup

GSM: Global Satellite for Mobile phone

Guguru: local popcorn

Guobodia Abel: A former Chair of Electoral Commission in Nigeria

H

Harmmattan: Dry cool season in the tropics

Hausa: The Hausa

Hiace: A brand of Toyota mini bus

I

Ibadan: Largest city in Africa, south of the sahara

Idiagbon: Second in Command to General Buhari when he was Head of State of Nigeria

Ife: Traditional Yoruba city

Igala: A language and people who live in and around Niger- Benue confluence in Kogi State of Nigeria

Igbo: The dominant ethnic group of South East Nigeria

Ijaw: A people in Niger Delta of Nigeria

Iroko: A hardwood tree found in the tropics believed to be coven of witches

Isiewu: An Igbo delicacy made from goat head

Iwu: A former Chair of Electoral Commission in Nigeria

J

Juju – fetish, voodoo

K

Kagasok: A kind of prophylactic drink made from the fermentation of yeast and some substance, said to have originated in Russia

Kampe: Pidgin for superb

Kokumo: Name given to an Abiku

Kpekere: Plantain chips

M

Majesties

Harnesses 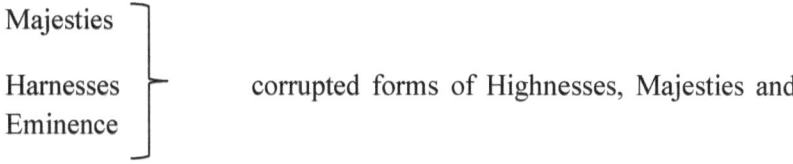 corrupted forms of Highnesses, Majesties and

Eminence

Eminences

Malam: Hausa for Mr.

Malomo: A Yoruba namefor an Abiku child

Marwa: A former Military Governor of Lagos State after whom the tricyle popularly used for transportation is named

Meaneaters: A corruption of ministers

Molue – mammy wagon common in Lagos

N

Na wetin: Pidgin expression meaning "what is it?"

Na wetin man pikin like to chop, na im de kill am: Pidgin expression meaning that a man is done in by his habits

Nupe: A language and People who dwell in and around

Nwosu Humphery: A former Chair of Electoral Commission in Nigeria

Nzeribe: A business man and politician associated with activities leading to the annulment of the Presidential elections of 1993 in Nigeria

O

Obe – chemicals poured into a river to kill fish

Odili Peter: A former Governor of Rivers State

Oduduwa : Yoruba ancestor

Ogbono – dika nuts made into sticky sauce

Ogegerugu – wooden framed mammy wagon

Oghene: Title of ruler of pre-Oduduwa Ife. Also mean God in some Edoid language groups

Ogiso : A dynasty of the ancient Benin Kingdom

Ogogoro: Local gin

Ogoni: A people who led the fight for environmental rights in the Niger Delta

Ogwugwu: Name of a juju shrine

Ohaneze: An Igbo socio-political group

Okija: A place in Eastern Nigeria that housed a juju shrine and local cult patronized by

Okunade Sijuade: An Ooni of Ife

Oloyin: sweet bean

Olubadan: The title of the king of Ibadan in Oyo State of Nigeria

Omo Ale: Yoruba for bastard

Omokomo: Yoruba for unruly child

Ondo: A state in South West Nigeria

Onilegogoro – Yoruba word for storied building, used for mini van with high roof

Onipangolo of Akitan: meaningless titular reference for vanity

Ooni: King of Ife

Oranmiyan: A Yoruba ancestor

Ora: A people in Owan West Local Government of Edo State

Ovie whisky: A former Chair of Electoral Commission in Nigeria

Owan: Name of a river and local government area in Edo State

Oyin: honey

R

Ritualists: Individuals involved in the use of human organs for fetish purposes

S

Saro Wiwa ken: Leader of Ogoni murdered by General Sanni Abacha

Sasa: A popular tomato market in Ibadan Nigeria

T

Tuwo: Rice semolina popular among the Hausa-Fulani

Tokunbo: Imported second hand or used item

U

Ule – Name of a stream in Oke, Owan East Local Government of Edo State, Nigeria

Uselu: A major road in Benin, Nigeria

W

Wahala: Trouble

Warantashi: An aphrodisiac

Werepe – Yoruba word for an itchy plant

Y

Yoruba: An ethnic group in south West Nigeria

Youth corper: Someone undertaking a mandatory year of National Service in Nigeria

Z

Zamfara: A state in North West Nigeria

Francis Egbokhare

www.ingramcontent.com/pod-product-compliance
Lightning Source LLC
Chambersburg PA
CBHW050444290526
45786CB00006B/2149